Quick Costumes for Kids

Quick Costumes for Kids

30 great fancy-dress ideas

Deborah House

hamlyn

To my family and friends for their
continuous love and support

First published in Great Britain in 2006 by
Hamlyn, a division of Octopus Publishing Group Ltd
2–4 Heron Quays, London E14 4JP

Distributed in the United States and Canada by
Sterling Publishing Co., Inc., 387 Park Avenue South,
New York, NY 10016–8810

ISBN-13: 978-0-600-61484-5
ISBN-10: 0-600-61484-0

A CIP catalogue record for this book is available
from the British Library

Printed and bound in China

10 9 8 7 6 5 4 3 2 1

Contents

Introduction

Even grown-ups enjoy fancy dress (or most of us do, anyway!). It's great fun, now and then, to pretend to be someone else and parade around in a magnificent or outlandish costume, or hide behind a mysterious mask.

For children – who have livelier imaginations and fewer inhibitions than grown-ups – the transformation of fancy dress is even more magical. You can help them live out their daydreams by making their favourite costumes from this book. Your little girl can become a shimmering fairy, dreamily dancing around in beautiful sequin-spangled net, or a Native American on the war path with tomahawk in hand. Her brother might be a fearsome pirate, on the prowl for treasure in striped top, eye patch and boots, or an elegant vampire with a swirling cape, dashing waistcoat and sharpened fangs.

Quick and easy

The costume-making process is designed to be simple, fast and fun. Once you've selected a costume, trace the relevant pattern pieces and templates from the pull-out sheet and template pages at the back of the book. (The templates on pages 140–43 are shown at 50 per cent and will need to be photocopied to enlarge them by 200 per cent to 100 per cent.) Assemble the required materials and equipment, which are all listed under each costume. Then follow the step-by-step instructions, referring, where necessary, to the introductory sections. 'Costume-making basics' (page 8) explains how to work with patterns and different fabrics. 'Sewing basics' (page 11) introduces simple techniques, from topstitching to making pompoms. 'Essential costumes' (page 14) shows how to make the basic costume shapes, such as a tunic or pair of wings, that are used for different outfits throughout the book.

The instructions for each costume include an estimate of how long it will take to make. If you are in a real hurry, follow the 'Time savers' advice for extra speed. Don't worry if you can't find all the materials suggested; you can probably find a substitute that will do just as well. Rummage around your house and in charity shops for inspiring and inexpensive objects that can be easily adapted to make costume props.

Little helpers

Children will enjoy the costumes even more if you get them involved in the creative process. Throughout the book, the 'Little helpers' tips suggest plenty of imaginative tasks that a child could do – or at least help with – such as making pompoms, masks and headdresses. Asking children to help choose fabrics and decorations is another easy way of letting them contribute to a project.

Enjoy making these costumes and seeing your child's imagination take flight. And don't forget to take some pictures!

Costume-making basics

The costumes in this book have been designed to fit children aged three to eight years old. Please refer to 'Measuring your child', right, before tracing the appropriate pattern from the pattern sheet. Note that fabric amounts given for each of the costumes are for size 7–8 years and allow for pattern pieces to be cut along the grain of the fabric, where relevant (see 'Understanding fabric', page 9). If making a costume in a smaller size, you may wish to buy slightly less fabric to avoid waste.

To use the pattern pieces you will need large sheets of tracing paper (available from art shops) and scissors for cutting paper (don't use dressmaking shears, as paper will blunt them). You'll also need masking tape and/or weights to hold the tracing paper in place and, of course, a pencil or pen. Make sure to transfer all the relevant marks onto each tracing.

For cutting out fabric pieces you will need dressmaker's pins (preferably the kind with large heads, which are less easily lost), ordinary dressmaker's shears, and pinking shears, which are specified for many patterns in the book. For small motifs, you may find it convenient to use special dressmaker's carbon paper. To use this, place the fabric right side up on a firm surface; place the paper, transfer side down, over it; and place the tracing, right side up, on top. Go over the lines firmly with a ball-point pen to transfer the motif shape onto the fabric. Cut out the fabric motif, using small, sharp-pointed scissors for details. When cutting out fur fabrics, you may prefer to draw around the pattern pieces, on the wrong side, rather than pinning them. Use tailor's chalk or a dressmaker's pencil, and hold the pattern in place with weights or a few pieces of masking tape.

Note Both metric and imperial measurements are given in this book. You can use either system, but stick to one system or the other; do not mix them!

Measuring your child

Before cutting out the pattern, measure your child using this diagram as a guide. Write down the measurements and keep them handy, so that, if necessary, you can adjust the pattern to fit the child.

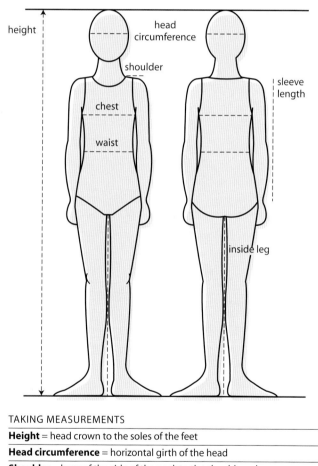

TAKING MEASUREMENTS

Height = head crown to the soles of the feet

Head circumference = horizontal girth of the head

Shoulder = base of the side of the neck to the shoulder edge

Chest = maximum girth measurement under the armpits and across the chest

Waist = waist girth with relaxed abdomen

Sleeve length = shoulder edge to the wrist

Inside leg = crotch to the soles of the feet

Understanding fabric

Most fabric is made by weaving threads together at right angles, although some is made by a knitting process. Knitted fabric is stretchy, whereas woven fabric has only a slight stretch along the bias – that is, the diagonal direction. The threads of a woven fabric – or the stitches and rows of a knitted one – are called the fabric's grain. The lengthways grain runs parallel to the fabric's selvedge (woven edge); the crosswise grain runs perpendicular to it. When making anything from fabric it's important to position the pattern pieces correctly relative to the grain, so that the pieces will hang well, or so that any design in the fabric will run correctly. For example, the centre front of a pattern piece is normally aligned with the lengthways grain. Words or symbols on the pattern piece indicate how that piece should be positioned.

For most patterns in this book, it does not matter whether the piece is placed on the right or wrong side of the fabric. Make sure, however, that any pattern piece that is asymmetrical and needs to be cut twice (such as the front of a waistcoat) is cut either on folded fabric or on a single layer with the pattern reversed for the second piece, so that you have two pieces that are mirror images of each other. Fabrics that are the same on both sides, such as felt and net, can be cut any way that is convenient.

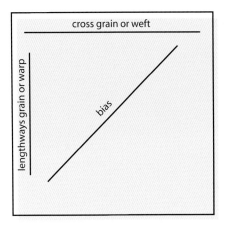

Cloth types

Different types of cloth have different properties. The main types of fabric used in this book are described below. If you cannot buy the fabric specified in one of the patterns, you could substitute a different type of cloth in a similar pattern or colour.

Cotton A natural fibre, which is cool, soft and comfortable to wear. It is absorbent and breathable and takes dye easily. It stands up to abrasion and washes and wears well. Many cotton fabrics are inexpensive and so are a good choice for children's garments.

Calico This coarse cloth is made from unbleached cotton, which is often only partially processed and therefore may contain parts of the husk. Due to its unfinished and undyed appearance, it is very inexpensive fabric, which can be used in its natural condition or dyed. Bleached calico is also available at a somewhat higher price.

Silk This is a luxurious and sensuous fabric which retains its shape and drapes well. This natural fibre is very strong and absorbent and so takes dye well, producing rich, intense colours.

Satin This smooth and shiny woven fabric, which can be made of silk or synthetic fibres, has a glossy, lustrous surface and a matt wrong side. The synthetic version is a cheaper alternative to silk but gives the same effect.

Fake fur A soft fabric which imitates real fur at a fraction of the price. When cutting, take care that the pile on the finished item will run in the correct direction; the pattern piece or instructions will specify this. (If you are cutting a detail such as a trim and wish to make a more economical use of fabric, simply brush the pile into the correct direction on the finished item.) You will find it easier to cut the pieces with the smooth wrong side up, holding the pattern in place with weights or masking tape and drawing around it.

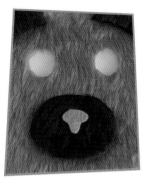

Marabou This is a soft, fluffy feather trimming, made from the down feathers of the marabou (a kind of stork).

Net This is an open fabric which is created by connecting intersections in a woven or knitted construction to form a mesh-like appearance. It is a transparent fabric which can be used to provide sheer layers which can also be easily ruched and gathered.

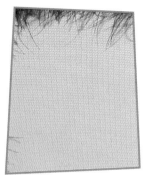

Felt This fabric is available in many colours but can also be obtained in a natural state, which is specially prepared for dyeing. It does not fray, which makes it a particularly easy fabric to work with, and it has no right or wrong side. Its soft quality is suitable for both hand and machine stitching.

Dyeing fabric

It is possible to buy special fabric dyes to use in the washing machine or, for hand-dyeing, in a large bowl. Dyeing is a good option if you cannot find fabric in the correct colour for the costume you wish to make; and it is recommended for some costumes in this book, as it gives a rustic look. However, commercially dyed fabric can be substituted, if necessary, for speed. When using dye, always read the manufacturers' instructions carefully, and protect your own clothing and skin.

Sewing basics

The costumes in this book require only basic sewing skills. It is advisable to use a sewing machine for speed, but the costumes can be hand-sewn if you prefer. Pinking shears are recommended for cutting fabrics that fray, as the edges do not need to be neatened. In some cases the pinked edges can be left raw to serve as a decorative feature.

Straight seams

A straight seam is made by placing at least two fabric pieces together with right sides facing and edges matching and then stitching through the layers in a straight line, at a specified distance from the raw edges – the seam allowance.

The seam allowances are normally pressed open unless otherwise stated in the instructions.

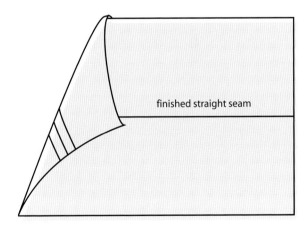

finished straight seam

Topstitching

As the name indicates, topstitching is worked on top of the fabric, by machine. It is often used in place of hand-hemming and to attach trimmings. Use straight stitch or zigzag stitch, as you like or as instructed.

Slipstitch

This hand stitch is used in many situations, often to close two opening edges after turning a section right side out. The seam allowances are turned in and pinned or tacked together. Take the needle under the seam allowance of the nearer fold, and fasten the thread with a few tiny stitches. Insert the needle into the opposite fold, just across from the starting point, and bring it out a short distance away through the nearer fold. Repeat.

Slipstitch can also be used to hem one edge over another. The basic method is the same, but the two pieces lie flat, with the overlapping section positioned above the other section.

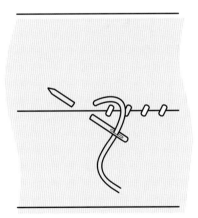

closing two edges

hemming one edge over another

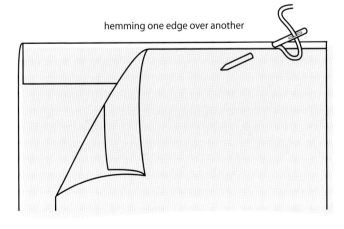

Gathers

1 Work two lines of stitching, 1 cm (³/₈ in) apart, using the longest stitch on the machine. Fasten the bobbin threads at one end by knotting them or winding them around a pin, then pull on the two bobbin threads at the other end (these are easier to pull than the top threads) until the edge is the required size. Fasten the bobbin threads as before.

2 Distribute the gathers evenly, then join the piece to the adjacent section as directed, stitching between the gathering threads. The outer gathering stitches can then be pulled out.

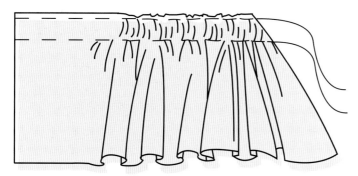

pull bobbin threads to gather fabric

Binding

1 Fold out one edge of bias binding and, with right sides together, pin edge of binding to edge of fabric, allowing a small amount of excess binding at each end. Stitch in place.

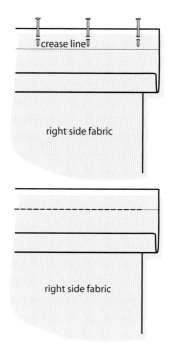

crease line

right side fabric

right side fabric

2 Fold remaining edge of binding to wrong side of fabric and turn under ends. Stitch in place.

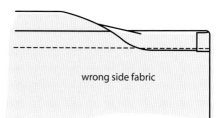

wrong side fabric

Pompoms

1 For a small pompom (such as Buzzy Bumble Bee's antennae), cut two cardboard discs approximately 6 cm (2$\frac{1}{4}$ in) in diameter. For a larger pompom (such as Floppy-eared Rabbit's tail), the diameter should be 10 cm (4 in). Cut a hole 1.5 cm ($\frac{5}{8}$ in) in diameter in one disc, then use this hole as a guide for marking and cutting a matching central hole in the other disc.

2 Place the discs together and wind yarn through and around until the centre hole is tightly packed. You'll need to use more than one length of yarn; knot the ends close to the hole and trim them. As the hole becomes full, you may need to thread the yarn into a large tapestry or yarn needle to pull it through. Hide the remaining end of yarn inside windings.

3 Insert scissors blade through the yarn, between the edges of the cardboard discs. Cut carefully all the way around the edges.

4 Pull the cards apart very slightly, and wrap a length of yarn between the discs around the middle of the yarn strands. Tie with a double knot. Leave a trailing end of yarn long enough for attaching the pompom. Fluff up the pompom and trim any protruding yarn ends.

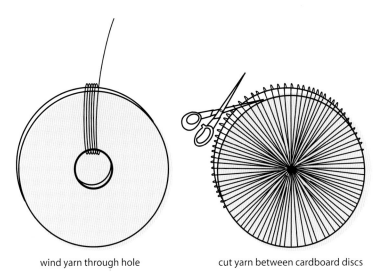

wind yarn through hole   cut yarn between cardboard discs

Making masks

Templates for masks shown in the book are given on pages 140–41 (reproduced at 50 per cent of actual size). Instructions for making masks are given with the relevant costumes. Each mask requires a piece of lightweight card and suitable fabric.

1 Trace the template, including the large face or head outline and the individual features, and photocopy to enlarge the template by 200 per cent, from 50 to 100 per cent. Cut the head piece from card and the relevant fabric, and the other pieces from specified fabrics. Glue them to the mask as directed for that costume.

2 When making a mask, be sure that it fits the child reasonably comfortably. Allow plenty of elastic to go around the head and adjust the length to fit. Before cutting the eye holes, try on the mask and ascertain the best position for the eyes. Alternatively, cut out the eye holes and then mark the best position for attaching the elastic, so that the mask won't slip down and obscure the child's vision.

Essential costumes

Tunic

Trim the front and back tunic pieces to the appropriate length for your child or for the costume. The tunic can be worn at ankle, mid-calf, knee or shirt length. Note that 1.5 cm ($^5/_8$ in) seam allowance has been included on both pattern pieces.

1. **Back-opening tunic** With fabric right sides together, folded in half (following lengthways grain, if any), pin on tunic (pattern 1), placing centre front on fold. Using pinking shears, cut a front piece. With fabric right side up, unfolded, pin on pattern and cut two back pieces, reversing pattern for a right and a left back piece. Pin on tunic sleeve (pattern 2) and cut two sleeves.

   Front-opening tunic With fabric right sides together, folded in half (following lengthways grain, if any), pin on tunic (pattern 1), placing centre back on fold. Using pinking shears, cut a back piece. With fabric right side up, unfolded, pin on pattern and cut two front pieces, reversing pattern for a right and a left front piece. Pin on tunic sleeve (pattern 2) and cut two sleeves.

2. Cut fabric according to pattern and child's height.

3. With right sides together, stitch sleeve to front and back fabric pieces along raglan edges. Repeat for second sleeve.

4. With right sides together, stitch centre back or centre front seam, leaving seam open above dot for neck opening (as shown in the illustration). Hem edges of neck opening.

5. With right sides together and raglan seams matching at underarm, stitch side and sleeve seams in a continuous process. Clip seam allowances at underarm point, almost to stitching. Press seam allowances open, and turn tunic right side out.

6. There are two basic ways of finishing the neck edge.
   With binding You can use either purchased binding (see page 12), which comes with two folded edges, or ribbon or a

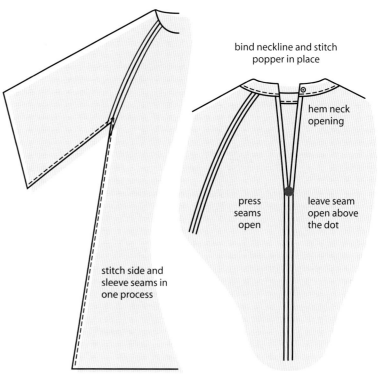

bind neckline and stitch popper in place

hem neck opening

press seams open

leave seam open above the dot

stitch side and sleeve seams in one process

strip of fabric. If using a strip of fabric, first fold under 1 cm ($^3/_8$ in) on the long edges. With right sides together and edges matching, pin binding around neck edge leaving a small amount of excess binding at each end. Stitch together along closer fold of binding. Turn remaining edge of binding inside neckline so that remaining folded edge of binding covers first line of stitching; turn under excess ends. Stitch in place, using straight or zigzag stitch or slipstitch. If using ribbon, simply fold it evenly over the neck edge, pin and tack it in place, then topstitch close to the ribbon edges.

Without binding Alternatively, you can omit the binding and simply turn under the neck edge and zigzag-stitch it. This method is recommended for some of the tunics that are covered by a cape or other garment.

7. Stitch popper in position. Press up seam allowance on sleeves and lower hem and stitch in place.

Trousers

Note that 1.5 cm (⅝ in) seam allowance has been included on pattern piece.

1 With fabric right sides together and folded in half, pin trouser piece (pattern 20) onto fabric and cut twice on the fold using pinking shears. Cut to desired length.

2 Fold both legs lengthways with right sides together and stitch inside leg seams.

3 Place one leg inside other, right sides facing. Stitch crotch seam from centre front to centre back, matching inside leg seams.

4 Turn under 4 cm (1½ in) on waist edge; stitch close to raw edge to form a casing. Unpick stitching on casing underside at centre back seam to make a small opening. Using a bodkin or large safety pin, thread 2.5 cm (1 in) wide elastic through the casing, allowing enough to fit child's waist minus 2 cm (¾ in). Stitch ends together and hand-stitch casing opening closed.

5 Turn under hems of trouser legs and stitch.

Waistcoat

Note that 1.5 cm (⅝ in) seam allowance has been included on all pattern pieces.

1 With fabric folded in half and right sides together, pin waistcoat piece (pattern 21) on the fold. Using pinking shears cut twice, to make two waistcoat backs.

2 Pin pattern onto double thickness of fabric (not on the fold) and cut twice, to make four fronts. Alternatively, cut one back and two fronts from lining fabric and the same number of each from the main fabric.

3 With right sides together, stitch main fabric front to back at shoulder seams; press seams open. Repeat for lining.

4 Pin waistcoat and lining together with right sides facing and edges and shoulder seams matching. Stitch along pinned edges, leaving side seams open. Trim stitched seam allowances and snip along curves so that fabric will lie flat. To turn waistcoat right side out, pull each front through the shoulder and out through one (not both) of the side seams. Press well, from the lining side, to bring seams to edge.

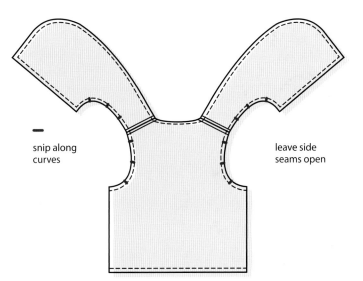

snip along curves

leave side seams open

5 With right sides together, stitch side seams of waistcoat only. Press seam open. (For a waistcoat with ties, see below.)

6 Smooth lining back over one side seam, clipping seam allowance at armhole and lower edge so that it will lie flat. Bring lining front side edge over seam and turn under seam allowance. Sew this to back lining using slipstitch.

Waistcoat with ties Cut two waistcoat ties, 38 x 4.5 cm (15 x 1¾ in). Fold each tie in half lengthways with right sides facing, and stitch along long side and across one end. Trim seam allowances and turn ties right side out; press. Pin each tie to waistcoat back, with raw edges matching, and topstitch in place, 4 cm (1½ in) from the edge. Join side seams as in steps 5 and 6 above.

Wings

1 Place wire on wing piece (pattern 11) and bend around shape until the outline is formed and the wires intersect. Twist wire together to secure. Without cutting, use remaining wire to mirror shape by following curves of first wing. Bend wings outwards to lie flat. Twist ends of wire around each other with pliers, and cut ends off with wire cutters.

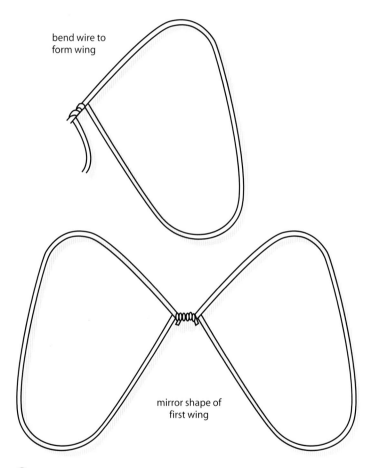

bend wire to
form wing

mirror shape of
first wing

2 Lay nylon net flat and place wire wings on top. Cut fabric so that it is 2 cm (³/₄ in) larger than wire form all around. Working on one wing at a time, apply craft glue around wire form and quickly stick fabric onto wire, taking care to keep fabric as smooth as possible. When glue has dried thoroughly, trim away excess fabric.

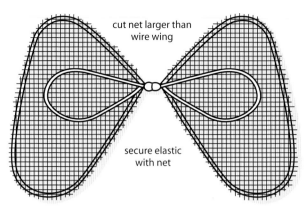

cut net larger than
wire wing

secure elastic
with net

3 Make even shoulder loops of elastic by knotting elastic ends together and placing on centre of join between wings. Secure elastic to wings by tightly binding with a scrap of net. Tie additional net around the join and form a bow.

4 Glue marabou around edge of wings on both sides.

Boots

Note that 1.5 cm (⁵/₈ in) seam allowance has been included on all pattern pieces.

1 Cut two uppers (pattern 47) for each foot (reversing to make two sides). Cut two soles (pattern 48), to make a left and a right.

2 With right sides together, stitch centre front open edge up to notch, as shown in illustration below. Stitch centre back seam.

3 With right sides together, stitch sole to underside of boots.

Animal boots Make paw soles (pattern 50) from contrasting felt. Stitch to uppers (pattern 49) as for ordinary boots.

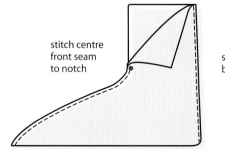

stitch centre
front seam
to notch

stitch centre
back seam

Animal mittens

Note that 1 cm (³/₈ in) seam allowance has been included on pattern piece.

1 Cut two pieces (pattern 51) from fur fabric, reversing to make a right and a left mitten. Cut two more from felt.

2 Glue contrasting felt paw pads on felt mitten. Stitch felt and fur, right sides together, leaving a gap at wrist. Turn right side out.

Hood (Rabbit and Dalmatian)

Note that 1.5 cm (⁵/₈ in) seam allowance has been included on all pattern pieces.

1 Pin hood crown (pattern 44) onto fur fabric and cut once with pinking shears. With fabric folded, right sides facing, cut one side piece (pattern 37) and two ears (pattern 43) on the fold.

2 With right sides together, stitch centre back seam of side piece to form a ring. Turn right side out.

3 With right sides together, stitch crown to side piece top edge.

4 With right sides together, stitch the two ear pieces together, leaving top edge open. Turn right side out.

5 With right sides together, stitch ear piece to lower edge of side piece, matching centre backs.

6 Turn under 1.5 cm (⁵/₈ in) on side piece edge, and zigzag-stitch.

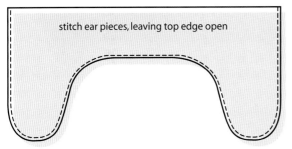

stitch ear pieces, leaving top edge open

Hood (Donkey, Teddy Bear and Big Bear)

Note that 1.5 cm (⁵/₈ in) seam allowance has been included on all pattern pieces.

1 With fabric right side up, pin crown (pattern 44) and ear pieces (pattern 41 or 42) onto appropriate fur fabric. Cut one crown and four ears (two front and two back) using pinking shears. With fabric right sides together and folded in half, cut one side piece (pattern 37) and two neck flaps (pattern 40).

2 With right sides together, stitch centre back seam of side piece to form a ring. Turn right side out.

3 With right sides together, stitch front and back ear pieces together, leaving bottom edge open; turn right side out.

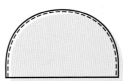

leave ear bottom edge open

4 Pin ears to inside of side piece either side of centre back seam. With right sides together, stitch crown to top edge of side piece, stitching ears in place at the same time.

5 Join the neck flaps, right sides together, leaving straight upper edge open. Clip curves and turn flap right side out. Place neck flap and lower side piece together, with centre back seam of side piece aligned with centre of flap. Stitch neck flap and side piece together. Turn flap down.

6 Turn under 1.5 cm (⁵/₈ in) on side piece edge, and zigzag-stitch in place.

Halloween

Wicked witch

She's scary, all right, but fun loving, too: under that cobweb-strewn black cape is a bright red satin lining and some flashy striped tights.

Equipment

- sewing machine
- sewing needle
- scissors
- pinking shears
- black and red thread
- pins
- craft glue
- face paints

Materials

Cape

1.5 m of 112 cm ($1^3/_4$ yd of 44 in) wide black satin

1.5 m of 112 cm ($1^3/_4$ yd of 44 in) wide red satin

3.5 cm ($1^1/_2$ in) wide red satin ribbon: 50 cm ($5/_8$ yd)

silver 3D glitter paint

1 popper fastener

Tunic

2 m of 112 cm ($2^1/_4$ yd of 44 in) wide black satin

red 1 cm ($3/_8$ in) wide bias binding: 50 cm ($5/_8$ yd)

1 popper fastener

Hat

50 cm of 112 cm ($5/_8$ yd of 44 in) wide black felt

3.5 cm ($1^1/_2$ in) wide red satin ribbon: 50 cm ($5/_8$ yd)

shirring elastic: 40 cm ($1/_2$ yd)

Ready-made items

striped tights

black nail varnish

black shoes (optional)

How quick?

3 hrs 30 mins

Time savers

Purchase witch hat.

Omit cobwebs on cape.

Omit red satin cape lining, and hem edges instead.

To make

Trace Wicked Witch patterns 1, 2, 22, 34 and 35 from pattern sheet, according to your child's age. Note that 1.5 cm ($^5/_8$ in) seam allowance has been included on all pattern pieces, apart from the hat, which has a 1 cm ($^3/_8$ in) seam allowance.

Cape

1 Fold black satin in half lengthways, with right sides facing. Pin cape piece (pattern 22) on fold and cut out using pinking shears. This piece is the back. From remaining black satin, cut two front cape pieces, not on the fold. Cut one with fabric right side up and one wrong side up, for a right and left front.

2 Cut identical pieces from red satin.

3 With right sides together, stitch black satin fronts to black satin back at side edges. Repeat with red satin pieces. Press seams open. Snip into curved edges to allow fabric to lie flat.

4 Pin black and red capes together with right sides facing. Stitch along front and lower edges, leaving neck edge open. Turn cape right side out.

5 Bind neck edge with red satin ribbon and then stitch popper in position.

6 Paint cobweb shapes onto cape using silver 3D glitter paint.

cape cobweb detail

Tunic

1 From black satin, make a basic tunic with back opening in the correct size (see page 14). Bind neckline with red bias binding.

2 Using pinking shears, trim sleeve edges and lower edge into jagged points.

Hat

1 Fold black felt in half lengthways. Pin hat pattern pieces on fold, and cut one crown (pattern 34) and two brims (pattern 35).

2 Stitch straight edges of crown together, taking 1 cm (³⁄₈ in) seam allowance. Press seam open and then turn crown right side out.

3 Stitch brim pieces together along outer edge. Turn brim right side out and press edges flat.

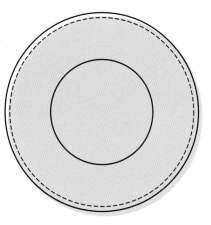

4 Pin and stitch crown to double inner edges of brim, taking 1 cm (³⁄₈ in) seam allowance.

5 Punch a hole on either side of crown. Thread shirring elastic through holes. Knot one end securely, try hat on child and adjust elastic for comfort. Knot remaining end and trim off any excess.

6 Glue red satin ribbon around base of crown.

Complete the outfit

Finish the costume with bold striped tights, a broomstick and black shoes (optional). Apply black nail varnish, and paint face and hands with green and black face paints.

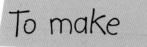

To make

Trace Wonderful Wizard templates from page 143 and photocopy to enlarge to 100 per cent. Trace patterns 1, 2, 34, 47 and 48 from pattern sheet, according to your child's age. Note that 1.5 cm (⁵/₈ in) seam allowance has been included on all pattern pieces.

Tunic

1 Make a basic tunic with a back opening in the correct size (see page 14). Bind the neckline with gold bias binding.

2 Using the templates on page 143, pin moon and star pieces onto the gold felt, and cut out as many shapes as desired. Save one felt star for the wizard hat.

3 Glue or stitch moon and star felt pieces onto the blue satin fabric in the desired arrangement.

Hat

1 Fold satin fabric in half lengthways with right sides facing. Pin hat piece (pattern 34) on fold, and cut out using pinking shears.

2 Place satin hat piece on card, and hold in position with straight pins. Draw around satin piece, then remove. Cut out card hat piece. Trim off 1 cm (³/₈ in) along curved edge of card.

turn in satin and glue

3 Glue or stitch gold felt star to centre of satin fabric so that it will sit at the front when hat is made up.

4 Stitch side edges of satin fabric together to form a cone shape. Lap one side edge of card shape over the other to form a cone a fraction smaller than the fabric cone. With a pencil, mark the position of the overlapping edge. Apply glue within the marked edge and stick edges together. Leave to dry.

5 Pull satin cone over cardboard cone, aligning seam with card edges. Turn edges of satin inside the cone and secure with glue.

6 Punch a hole on either side of hat edge. Thread shirring elastic through holes. Knot one end securely, try hat on child and adjust elastic for comfort. Knot remaining end and trim off excess.

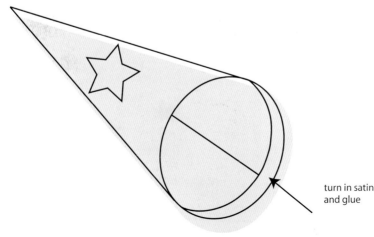

Boots

Make a pair of basic boots (see page 16).

Staff

1 Spray twig/bamboo stick with silver spray paint. Allow to dry.

2 Gouge a hole into the cotton ball and insert twig. Glue to secure. Add glitter to ball if desired.

3 Wind gold/silver chenille sticks around the twig and cotton ball to secure the ball. Wind blue sticks around the twig.

Complete the outfit

Add purchased wizard beard, moustache and glasses.

Magic black cat

This easy costume consists of ears, tail and furry chest, teamed with basic wardrobe pieces. Face paints will give your little black cat bewitching feline features.

Equipment

sewing machine

sewing needle

scissors

pinking shears

black and white thread

pins

wire cutters

craft glue

safety pin

face paints

Materials

Ears

velvet-covered Alice band

10 cm of 112 cm ($^1/_8$ yd of 44 in) wide black stretch velour

10 cm of 112 cm ($^1/_8$ yd of 44 in) wide thin polyester wadding

6 cm ($2^1/_2$ in) white marabou trim

Fur chest

40 cm of 112 cm ($^1/_2$ yd of 44 in) wide white fur fabric

1 popper fastener

Tail

piece of black stretch velour, 38 cm (lengthways grain) x 12 cm (15 x 5 in)

piece of thin polyester wadding, 38 x 12 cm (15 x 5 in)

piece of white fur fabric, 5 x 5 cm (2 x 2 in), or 5 cm (2 in) of white marabou

1.6 mm diameter (14 gauge) galvanized tie wire: 30 cm (12 in)

Ready-made items

black leotard

black leggings

black shoes (optional)

How quick?

1 hr 20 mins

Time savers

Purchase black ears and tail from a fancy-dress shop.

For a sleeker look, omit fur chest piece.

Little helpers

Your little cat will enjoy applying face paints. Let her smudge pink paint onto her little nose before you help out with the trickier application of painted black whiskers.

To make

Trace Magic Black Cat patterns 26, 27 and 28 from pattern sheet, according to your child's age and height. Note that 1.5 cm ($\frac{5}{8}$ in) seam allowance has been included on all pattern pieces, apart from the ear, which has a 1 cm ($\frac{3}{8}$ in) seam allowance.

Ears

1 Fold black stretch velour double, wrong sides facing, and cut four ear pieces (pattern 27), using pinking shears. Make sure nap always slopes the same way. Cut two ears from wadding.

2 Place two velour ear pieces together with right sides facing, then place a wadding piece on top. Stitch around the curved edges only. Trim seam allowances to 5 mm ($\frac{1}{4}$ in) and turn ear right side out. Trim the wadding slightly along the opening edges. Turn velour edges inside and slipstitch together. Repeat to make other ear.

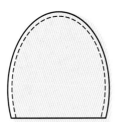
leave lower edge open

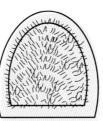
glue on marabou

3 Cut piece of white marabou in half. Glue each half onto front of ear shapes and leave to dry. Hand-stitch or glue onto black velvet Alice band.

Fur chest

1 With fabric right side up, pin chest piece (pattern 26) onto white fur fabric. Cut two pieces using pinking shears, positioning the pattern pieces so that the pile slants away from the centre front on each.

2 Place chest pieces together with right sides facing. Stitch and press centre seam open. Turn under a narrow hem on remaining edges and hand-stitch in place.

3 Stitch popper in position.

Tail

1 Fold black stretch velour in half lengthways with right sides facing. Place tail piece (pattern 28) on fold, pin to fabric, and cut out using pinking shears.

2 With fabric still folded, stitch long edges and narrow end of tail together. Trim seam allowance to 5 mm (¹/₄ in). Turn tail right side out.

3 Cover the wire with wadding and glue wadding edges together. Pull velour tail over wadding. Trim wadding slightly, fold in velour edges and slipstitch together. Wrap white marabou or fur fabric around tip of tail, and stitch or glue in place. Add a safety pin to the other end of the tail in order to secure tail to costume. Bend tail into desired position.

pull velour over wadding

Complete the outfit

Finish the costume with leggings and leotard. Before painting on her cat face, add ears, chest and tail. *Mee-ow!*

wrong side

turn under a
narrow hem
and stitch

right
sides
together

pile

stitch along
centre seam

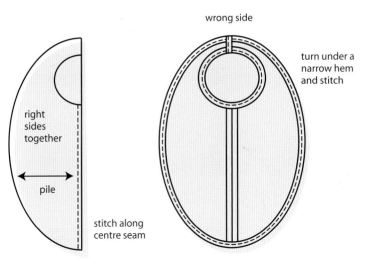

Fang-tastic vampire

This bloodthirsty denizen of the night is a chilling sight, with his ghostly white face and bat-encrusted cape – not to mention those vampire teeth.

Equipment

sewing machine

sewing needle

scissors

pinking shears

black, red and grey thread

pins

craft glue

face paints and hair gel

Materials

Cape

1.5 m of 112 cm (1¼ yd of 44 in) wide black satin

1.5 m of 112 cm (1¼ yd of 44 in) wide red satin

40 cm of 112 cm (½ yd of 44 in) wide black felt, or 5 squares, 30 x 30 cm (12 x 12 in)

piece of collar stiffener, or extra-heavy interfacing, 25 x 55 cm (10 x 22 in)

2.5 cm (1 in) wide black velvet ribbon: 40 cm (½ yd)

pendant

small square of black Velcro

Waistcoat

1.2 m of 112 cm (⅝ yd of 44 in) wide grey or beige jacquard fabric

1.2 m of 112 cm (⅝ yd of 44 in) wide red lining fabric

4 large black buttons

3 popper fasteners

Bow tie

20 cm of 112 cm (¼ yd of 44 in) wide red satin

shirring elastic

Trousers

1.5 m of 112 cm (1¾ yd of 44 in) wide closely woven black cotton

2.5 cm (1 in) wide elastic: 50 cm (⅝ yd)

Ready-made items

white shirt

black shoes

vampire teeth

How quick?
3 hrs 30 mins

Time savers

Use child's own black trousers.

Omit waistcoat or use ready-made item.

Omit red satin lining and hem cape edges instead.

Little helpers
Your child can decorate the bats and glue them onto the cape himself.

To make

Trace Fang-tastic Vampire templates from pages 142–3 and photocopy to enlarge to 100 per cent. Trace patterns 20, 21 and 25 from pattern sheet, according to your child's age. Note that 1.5 cm ($^5/_8$ in) seam allowance has been included on all pattern pieces where appropriate.

Cape

1 From black satin, cut a rectangle 83 cm (33 in) long (lengthways grain) across the whole width of the fabric. Repeat with the red satin. Place the two pieces together with right sides facing and stitch together along one long and two short sides. Turn cape right side out.

2 Using remaining black satin, folded on lengthways grain, pin collar piece (pattern 25) on fold and cut out. Repeat with red satin. Cut another collar piece from collar stiffener.

3 Stitch or glue collar stiffener to wrong side of red collar piece. Place black piece on red piece with right sides facing. Stitch collar pieces together at side and top edges, leaving neck edge open. Trim seam allowances close to stitching, and turn collar right side out.

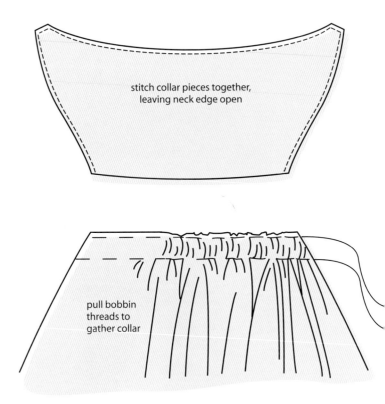

stitch collar pieces together, leaving neck edge open

pull bobbin threads to gather collar

4 Using the longest machine stitch, work two lines of stitching, 1 cm ($^3/_8$ in) apart, across the raw edges of the cape, through both layers. Pull up bobbin threads so that cape fits collar neck edge, and knot them together. Adjust gathers evenly.

5 Place cape and collar together with black sides facing. Pin securely, leaving stiffened red side of collar free, and machine-stitch in place.

6 Turn under free edge of red collar lining and slipstitch to red lining of cape.

7 Fold black velvet ribbon in half crossways, with right sides facing. Stitch a tiny dart over fold, so that ribbon will form a slight angle when opened flat. Stitch one half of Velcro to right-hand end of velvet ribbon; stitch other half to right-hand edge of cape at neckline. Topstitch left-hand end of ribbon to left side of cape at neckline. Stitch pendant to point of ribbon.

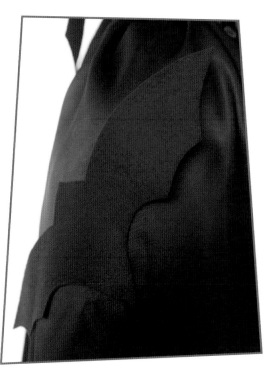

Bat decorations

1. Using the template on page 143, pin the bat cape detail to the black felt and cut around the shape. Repeat to make as many bats as desired.

2. Decorate the bats as you wish. For example, sequins could be glued onto the shapes to suggest bat eyes.

3. Glue each decorated bat body onto cape, leaving wings unglued to create a 3D effect.

Waistcoat

1 Using grey or beige jacquard fabric and lining fabric, make a basic waistcoat with ties (see page 15).

2 Stitch three popper fasteners at centre front where indicated on pattern piece.

3 Stitch four black buttons onto front of waistcoat where indicated on pattern piece.

Bow tie

1 Using the templates on page 142, pin bow tie pieces to red satin fabric, with fabric right side up, and cut once using pinking shears.

2 Fold in edges of bow section and centre tie as indicated. Pull centre tie around centre of bow section in order to form a bow shape. Stitch or glue ends of centre tie together at back of bow.

3 Cut shirring elastic to fit neck of purchased shirt. Stitch ends of elastic to back of bow tie.

Trousers

From black cotton, make a pair of basic trousers (see page 15).

Complete the outfit

Finish the costume with a white shirt and black shoes, then let your child enjoy painting a ghostly white face and blood-stained lips with face paints. Apply hair gel to create a sleek look and insert vampire teeth for a real fright.

Terrifying ghost

This simple costume gives you lots of shivers for very little time and money. Just make sure that the mask fits your child well, so the ghost can see where it's haunting.

Equipment

sewing machine
sewing needle
scissors
pinking shears
white thread
pins
black felt-tip pen
craft glue

Materials

Tunic

2 m of 140 cm (2¼ yd of 55 in) wide
  white cotton
1 popper fastener

Mask

piece of lightweight card, 30 x 30 cm
  (12 x 12 in)
piece of white felt, 30 x 30 cm
  (12 x 12 in)
shirring elastic: 30 cm (12 in)

How quick?
2 hrs

Time savers

Omit hood.
Use a purchased mask.

Little helpers

Children may want to make
their own masks.

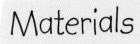

To make

Trace Terrifying Ghost template from page 140 and photocopy to enlarge to 100 per cent. Trace patterns 1, 2 and 30 from pattern sheet, according to your child's age. Note that 1.5 cm (⁵/₈ in) seam allowance has been included on all pattern pieces.

Hooded tunic

1 From white cotton make a basic tunic with front opening (see page 14). Leave neck opening unstitched.

2 From remaining white cotton, cut two hood pieces (pattern 30) with pinking shears: one with fabric right side up and one with it wrong side up, so you have a right and a left hood.

3 Place hood pieces together with right sides facing, and stitch down the centre back. Snip curved edges of seam allowance and press seam open.

4 Pin neck edges of hood and tunic together with right sides facing and centre back seam of hood at centre back of tunic. Stitch neck seam. Snip curves to allow fabric to lie flat.

5 Turn under seam allowance of hood front edge and tunic neck opening, and stitch.

6 Stitch popper at centre front neck opening as indicated on pattern piece.

7 Using pinking shears, trim sleeve edges and lower edge into jagged points.

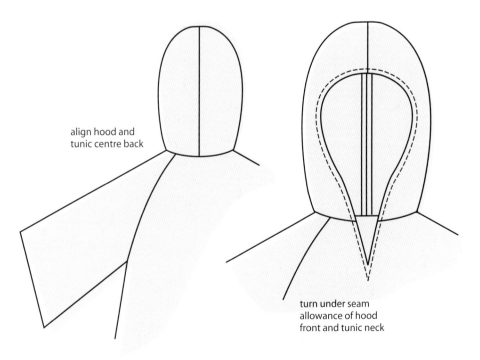

align hood and tunic centre back

turn under seam allowance of hood front and tunic neck

Mask

1 Using template on page 140, cut two ghost mask pieces: one from card and one from white felt. Glue felt piece to card piece. Allow to dry.

2 Punch a hole on either side of mask. Thread shirring elastic through holes. Knot one end securely, try mask on child and adjust elastic for comfort. Knot remaining end and trim off excess.

3 Try mask on child again and, using felt-tip pen, gently mark two dots for centres of eye holes. Remove mask. Using a coin of appropriate size as a template, draw eye holes. Draw on spooky eye sockets, using the template on page 140 as a guide. Fill in with black felt-tip pen. Cut out eye holes. Add two nostrils with felt-tip pen.

Scary skeleton

'Them bones gonna walk around . . .' – and very soon, too! Just glue them onto your child's black top, leggings and gloves, then run and hide behind the sofa!

Equipment

scissors
pins
craft glue
face paints

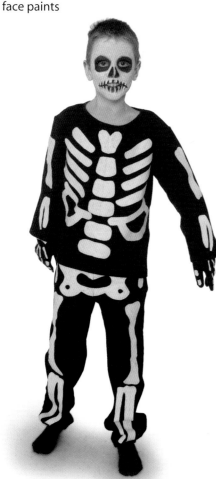

Materials

Bones

1 m of 112 cm ($1\frac{1}{8}$ yd of 44 in) wide white felt

Ready-made items
black top
black leggings
black gloves
black shoes (optional)
skeleton mask

How quick?

1 hr 20 mins

Time saver

Buy ready-made bone stickers.

Little helpers

Your little helper can design a spooky skeleton face for you to re-create with face paints.

To make

Trace Scary Skeleton patterns 52, 53, 54, 55, 56, 57 and 58 from pattern sheet, according to your child's age.

Bones

1 Pin bone pattern pieces onto double thickness white felt. Cut pelvis piece and all vertebrae on the fold. Cut two pieces of all other bones (not cutting on the fold).

2 Using photographs as a guide and referring to chest and hand layouts (patterns 52 and 55), glue bones onto black top, leggings and black gloves.

Complete the outfit

Finish with purchased skeleton mask, or apply black and white face paints. Add black shoes, if desired.

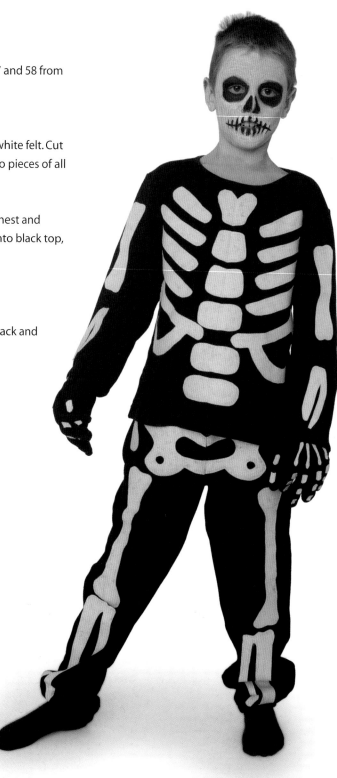

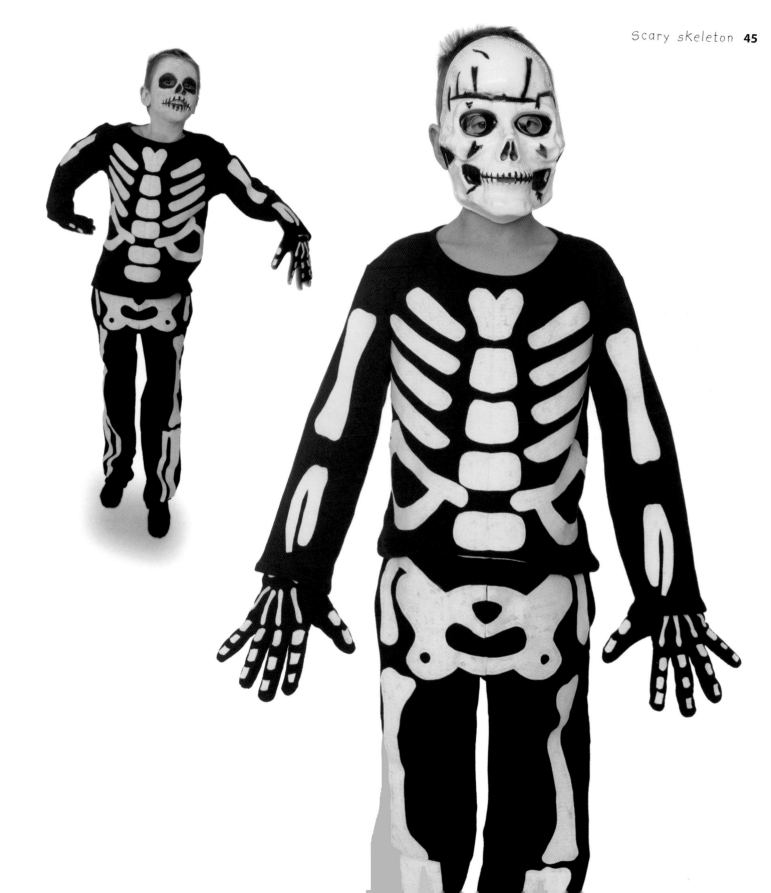

Mary and Joseph

The two main Christmas characters have easy costumes. Basic tunics in dyed calico are decorated with braid and teamed with simple headdresses for a biblical effect.

Equipment

sewing machine

sewing needle

scissors

pinking shears

blue and brown thread

pins

large container for dyeing fabric

Materials

Mary

Tunic

2 m of 112 cm (2¼ yd of 44 in) wide unbleached calico

white rickrack: 2.3 m (2½ yd)

white 1 cm (½ in) wide bias binding: 50 cm (⅝ yd)

rope, 1.5 m (1¾ yd)

1 popper fastener

blue fabric dye

Headdress

1 m of 112 cm (1⅛ yd of 44 in) wide pure white calico

Wrap for baby doll

1 m of 112 cm (1⅛ yd of 44 in) wide pure white calico

Ready-made items

baby doll

sandals (optional)

Joseph

Tunic

2.7 m of 112 cm (3 yd of 44 in) wide unbleached calico (includes fabric for headdress)

white rickrack: 2.3 m (2½ yd)

cream 1 cm (⅜ in) wide bias binding: 50 cm (⅝ yd)

rope, 1.5m (1¾ yd)

1 popper fastener

brown fabric dye

Headdress

piece of dyed-brown calico, 75 x 112 cm (30 x 44 in), cut from tunic fabric

white 5 cm (2 in) wide braid: 80 cm (⅞ yd); or strip of white fabric twice this width

Coat

1 m of 140 cm (1⅛ yd of 55 in) wide striped taffeta or furnishing fabric

cream 1 cm (½ in) wide bias binding: 50 cm (⅝ yd)

1 popper fastener

Ready-made items

false beard

sandals (optional)

How quick?

Mary 2 hrs (not including time
for fabric dye to dry)
Joseph 2 hrs 45 mins
(not including time
for fabric dye to dry)

Time savers

Leave edges of fabric raw for a
more homespun look.

Omit Joseph's coat.

Use pre-dyed fabric.

To make

Trace Mary and Joseph patterns 1 and 2 from pattern sheet, according to your child's age. Note that 1.5 cm (⁵/₈ in) seam allowance has been included on all pattern pieces.

Tunics

1. Dye smaller piece of unbleached calico with blue fabric dye and larger piece with brown fabric dye, following the manufacturers' instructions. Leave fabric to dry. Cut off 75 cm (30 in) of brown fabric and set aside for headdress.

2. Using the blue and brown calico, cut pieces for two basic tunics with back opening (see page 14).

3. Before joining the tunic seams, stitch rickrack onto edges of sleeves and hem as shown in photograph.

4. Complete tunics, following basic tunic instructions and using the white/cream bias binding to finish the neck edges.

Headdresses

1. **Mary** For Mary's headdress, turn under and stitch edges of pure white calico.

2. **Joseph** For Joseph's headdress, pink edges of remaining rectangle of brown dyed calico.

3. If using fabric strip to fasten headdresses, seam long edges of strip and one short end. Turn strip right side out. Tuck in raw edges and stitch to close.

Joseph's coat

1 Using striped taffeta, make a basic tunic with front opening (see page 14).

2 Hem centre front seam and bind neckline with cream bias binding. Stitch popper as indicated on pattern piece.

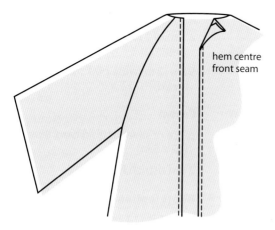

hem centre
front seam

Complete the outfit

Finish tunics by tying rope around waist. Give Joseph his false beard. Fasten headdresses by tying braid or fabric strip around head. Alternatively, Mary's headdress can be fastened at nape of neck with a safety pin, as shown in the picture. Sandals can be worn, if desired. Wrap the baby doll in piece of white cloth.

To make

Wise Man 1

Trace Wise Man 1 patterns 1, 2, 36, 47 and 48 from pattern sheet, according to your child's age. Note that 1.5 cm (⁵⁄₈ in) seam allowance has been included on all pattern pieces.

Tunic

1 From blue cotton, cut pieces for a basic tunic with back opening (see page 14).

2 Before joining the tunic seams, glue or stitch pink ribbon to sleeves as shown in photograph.

3 Complete tunic, following basic tunic instructions and using the pink ribbon to bind the neck edges.

Coat

1 Fold striped silk in half lengthways, with right sides facing. Pin back piece (pattern 1) on fold and cut out with pinking shears. From remaining striped silk, cut two front pieces (pattern 1), not on the fold – one with fabric right side up and one with it wrong side up, for a right and left front.

2 With right sides together stitch fronts to back at shoulder and side edges. Turn coat right side out.

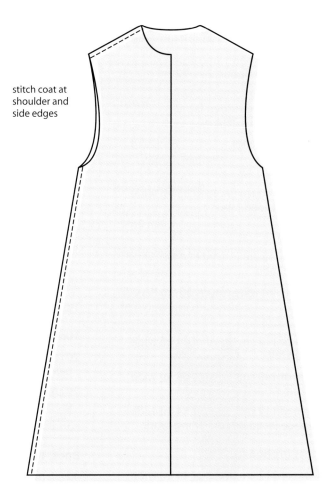

stitch coat at shoulder and side edges

3 Bind neckline with pink ribbon.

4 Turn under and stitch a small hem around armholes and along lower and centre front edges.

Waist sash

Turn under edges of pink silk and hem with zigzag stitch.

Crown

1 Cut crown (pattern 36) from silver or gold card.

2 Overlap edges (check size on child) and glue them together. Glue ostrich feathers to inside front edge of crown.

Boots

Using blue felt, make a pair of basic boots (see page 16).

Complete the outfit

Tie pink sash around costume as shown in picture and secure with a knot.

To make

Wise Man 2

Trace Wise Man 2 patterns 1, 2, 20, 37, 38, 39, 44, 47 and 48 from pattern sheet, according to your child's age. Note that 1.5 cm (5/8 in) seam allowance has been included on all pattern pieces.

Tunic

1 From purple satin, cut out pieces for a basic tunic with back opening (see page 14).

2 Cut piece of green fabric in half lengthways; repeat with purple striped fabric. Zigzag-stitch one strip of purple striped fabric to centre of each strip of green fabric.

3 Before stitching sleeve seams, zigzag-stitch or glue green and purple striped bands to sleeve hems as shown in illustration.

4 Complete tunic, following basic tunic instructions, but simply turning under and hemming the neck edge.

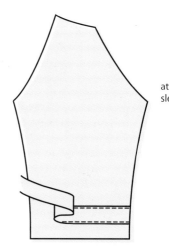

attach striped bands to sleeve hems

Sash

Fold the striped fabric in half lengthways, right sides together, and stitch long edges and one short end. Trim seam and turn sash right side out. Turn in raw edges and stitch.

Trousers

From purple satin, make a pair of basic trousers (see page 15).

Hat

1 Fold green felt and striped fabric double. Cut one striped brim (pattern 38) and one green side piece (pattern 37) on the fold, and one green crown (pattern 44) not on the fold, using pinking shears.

2 From orange jacquard fabric, cut four hat flap pieces (pattern 39), using pinking shears.

3 With right sides together, stitch short ends of green side piece to form a ring. Turn right side out.

4 With right sides together, stitch crown to side piece.

5 Pin one flap piece to another, matching the right side of one to the wrong side of the other, so that the wrong side of the fabric will show on the lining. Stitch around three edges, leaving narrow top edge open. Trim seam and turn flap right side out. Repeat with remaining two flap pieces.

6 Stitch ends of brim piece together to form a ring.

7 Fold brim in half lengthways. Pin brim edges to side piece, incorporating flaps at same time. Stitch through all layers, taking a 1 cm ($^3/_8$ in) seam allowance. Turn back brim.

Boots

Using green felt, make a pair of basic boots (see page 16).

Complete the outfit

Tie purple striped sash around tunic waist and knot to secure.

To make

Wise Man 3

Trace Wise Man 3 patterns 1, 2, 20, 21, 47 and 48 from pattern sheet, according to your child's age. Note that 1.5 cm ($^5/_8$ in) seam allowance has been included on all pattern pieces.

Tunic

From pale green brocade, make a basic tunic with back opening (see page 14). Turn under and stitch the neck edges.

Waistcoat

From green furnishing fabric, make a basic waistcoat (see page 15), omitting the ties.

Trousers

1 From green satin, make a pair of basic trousers (see page 15).

2 Turn under 2 cm ($^3/_4$ in) on lower edges of trousers and stitch close to the raw edge, leaving a 3 cm (1$^1/_4$ in) gap. Thread elastic through casings and tie ends in a double knot. Stitch the gap closed.

Turban

Stitch the strip of pale green brocade and the strip of furnishing fabric together along one long edge. Then press seam open. Neaten the remaining raw edges with close zigzag stitch.

Boots

Using green felt, make a pair of basic boots (see page 16).

Complete the outfit

To finish dressing the child, wrap turban fabric around head as shown in the photograph, and secure with one or more safety pins. Sew tassel to back of turban. Tie thick curtain cord with tassels around waist to make a belt.

Heavenly angel

Pure white cotton embellished with gold ribbon and marabou wings will make your child look angelic, whatever she gets up to!

Equipment

- sewing machine
- sewing needle
- scissors
- pinking shears
- white and gold thread
- pins
- wire cutters
- pliers
- craft glue

Materials

Tunic

2 m of 112 cm (2¼ yd of 44 in) wide white cotton

3.5 cm (1½ in) wide gold ribbon: 5 m (5½ yd)

1 popper fastener

shirring elastic

Wings

60 cm of 112 cm (¾ yd of 44 in) wide white nylon net

white marabou trim: 2 m (2¼ yd)

1.6 mm diameter (14 gauge) galvanized tie wire: 1 m (1⅛ yd)

white 1 cm (⅜ in) wide elastic: 1 m (1⅛ yd)

Halo

Alice band, 6–10 mm (¼–⅜ in) wide

3.5 cm (1½ in) wide gold ribbon: 80 cm (⅞ yd)

1 extra-long white chenille stick

How quick?

2 hrs 40 mins

Time saver

Purchase white wings.

Little helpers

Your little angel can try adding different types of gold or silver decoration to her halo.

To make

Trace Heavenly Angel patterns 1, 2 and 11 from pattern sheet, according to your child's age and height. Note that 1.5 cm ($^5/_8$ in) seam allowance has been included on all pattern pieces.

Tunic

1 From white cotton, cut out pieces for a basic tunic with back opening (see page 14).

2 Before sewing pieces together, stitch or glue gold ribbon along hem and sleeves, as shown in the photograph. Use the gold ribbon to bind the neckline.

3 Complete tunic, following basic tunic instructions. Zigzag-stitch two rows of shirring elastic just below chest level, where indicated in the illustration below.

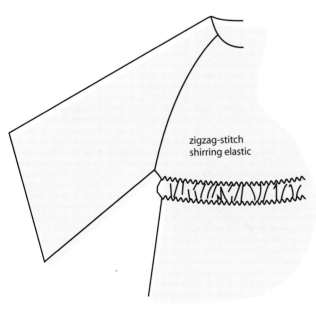

zigzag-stitch
shirring elastic

4 Tie remaining gold ribbon around shirring elastic, and secure in a bow at the back.

Wings

Using tie wire, marabou and net, make a pair of wings (see page 16).

Halo

1 Measure length of Alice band and cut a piece of gold ribbon to this length plus 2.5 cm (1 in). Fold ribbon in half lengthways with right sides together. Slip it over Alice band to check fit. Stitch long edges together, taking care not to exceed possible seam allowance and providing for some ease. Stitch across one end, taking 1 cm ($^3/_8$ in) seam allowance. Turn ribbon right side out (a knitting needle is helpful for this). Pull ribbon over Alice band, turn in raw edges, and slipstitch together.

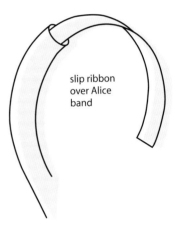

slip ribbon over Alice band

2 Make a halo out of white chenille stick by bending one end into a circle, turning other end perpendicular, and twisting straight end around the Alice band. Wrap gold ribbon around chenille stick to add sparkle, and secure with hand stitches or glue.

Lively donkey

No Nativity scene is complete without Mary and Joseph's donkey. This endearing animal has a floppy tail and a thick, shaggy mane.

Equipment

- sewing machine
- sewing needle
- scissors
- pinking shears
- grey thread
- pins
- craft glue

Materials

Fur top

1.5 m of 140 cm (1¾ yd of 55 in) wide grey fur fabric

1 popper fastener

Mane

50 cm of 140 cm (⅝ yd of 55 in) wide black shaggy fur fabric

Trousers

1.5 m of 140 cm (1¾ yd of 55 in) wide grey fur fabric

2.5 cm (1 in) wide elastic: 50 cm (⅝ yd)

Mittens

40 cm of 140 cm (½ yd of 55 in) wide black shaggy fur fabric

Tail

30 cm of 140 cm (⅜ yd of 55 in) wide grey fur fabric

piece of black shaggy fur fabric 10 x 10 cm (4 x 4 in)

piece of thin wadding, 30 x 30 cm (12 x 12 in)

Boots

40 cm of 140 cm (½ yd of 55 in) black shaggy fur fabric

piece of black felt, 28 x 28 cm (11 x 11 in)

Mask (optional)

piece of lightweight card, 30 x 24 cm (12 x 9½ in)

piece of grey fur fabric, 30 cm (in direction of pile) x 24 cm (12 x 9½ in)

piece of black shaggy fur fabric, 20 x 10 cm (8 x 4 in)

scrap of black felt

shirring elastic: 30 cm (⅜ yd)

Hood (optional)

50 cm of 140 cm (⅝ yd of 55 in) wide grey fur fabric

piece of black shaggy fur fabric, 20 x 10 cm (8 x 4 in)

How quick?

2 hrs 40 mins

Time saver

Omit mittens and boots.

Little helpers

Helping to create a mask will keep little donkeys amused for hours.

To make

Trace Lively Donkey template from page 140 and photocopy to enlarge to 100 per cent. Trace patterns 1, 2, 20, 28, 37, 40, 41, 44, 49, 50 and 51 from pattern sheet, according to your child's age and height. Note that 1.5 cm ($^5/_8$ in) seam allowance has been included on all pattern pieces, apart from the mitten, which has a 1 cm ($^3/_8$ in) seam allowance.

Fur top

1 From grey fur fabric, make a basic tunic with back opening (see page 14). Leave the centre back edges open. Turn under and zigzag-stitch the neck and lower edge.

2 From black shaggy fur fabric cut a piece 61 x 23 cm (24 x 9 in) to create a mane. Fold fabric in half lengthways with right sides facing. Stitch together along one short end and remaining long side. Cut diagonally across stitched corners to reduce bulk, and turn mane right side out. Topstitch remaining short end.

3 Glue mane to centre back seam.

4 Attach popper fastener at neck opening.

Mittens

1 Place black fur fabric right side up, and cut two animal mitten pieces (pattern 51). Turn the pattern piece over and cut two more, so that you have two right pieces and two left pieces.

2 Placing right sides together, stitch the two right pieces together around curved edge. Repeat with left pieces. Trim seams close to stitching and turn right side out.

Trousers

From grey fur fabric, make a pair of basic trousers (see page 15). Leave a 6 cm (2½ in) gap at the seat for inserting tail.

Tail

1 Fold grey fur fabric in half lengthways, pin tail (pattern 28) on fold and cut out using pinking shears.

2 With tail still folded, stitch around edges of shape, leaving the end open. Turn tail right side out.

3 Fold black shaggy fur piece in half, right sides together, along the pile. Stitch close to the edge. Turn piece right side out, slip it over the end of the tail and glue or stitch in place.

4 Turn trousers wrong side out. Insert free end of tail in the gap and stitch in place through all thicknesses.

Boots

From black shaggy fur and black felt (for soles), make a pair of basic boots (see page 16).

Mask (optional)

1 Using template on page 140, cut the following pieces: one head piece from lightweight card; one head piece from grey fur fabric (with pile lengthways); a right and a left ear centre from black shaggy fur fabric; a mane from black shaggy fur fabric. Cut two dots of black felt for nostrils.

2 Glue fur head piece to card head piece. Allow to dry. Glue on other features, and allow to dry.

3 Punch a hole on either side of mask. Thread shirring elastic through holes. Knot one end securely, try mask on child and adjust elastic for comfort. Knot remaining end and trim off any excess.

4 Try mask on child again and, using felt-tip pen, gently mark two dots for centres of eye holes. Remove mask. Using a coin of appropriate size as a template, draw eye holes; cut out.

Hood (optional)

Cut out pieces for a donkey hood (see page 17) from grey fur fabric, using black shaggy fur fabric for two of the ear pieces.

1 For the mane, cut a piece of black shaggy fur 33 x 23 cm (13 x 9 in) across the fabric. Fold mane in half lengthways, with right sides facing. Stitch across one short end and adjacent long side. Clip seam allowances, and trim diagonally across stitched corners. Turn mane right side out and topstitch remaining short end.

2 Complete the hood (see page 17).

3 Glue mane to centre back seam.

Party

Colourful clown

The bright, cheerful colours of this outfit can be mixed and matched to create an exciting costume for a boy or girl.

Equipment

sewing machine

sewing needle

scissors

pinking shears

yellow and pink thread

pins

wire cutters

craft glue

face paints

Materials

Baggy trousers

2 m of 112 cm ($2^1/_4$ yd of 44 in) wide bright yellow satin

40 cm of 112 cm ($^1/_2$ yd of 44 in) wide pink felt, or 4 squares, 30 x 30 cm (12 x 12 in)

1 cm ($^3/_8$ in) wide elastic: 1.2 m ($1^3/_8$ yd)

Braces

30 cm of 112 cm ($^3/_8$ yd of 44 in) wide bright yellow satin

20 cm of 112 cm ($^1/_4$ yd of 44 in) wide pink felt, or 2 squares, 30 x 30 cm (12 x 12 in)

2 cm ($^3/_4$ in) wide elastic: 1.2 m ($1^3/_8$ yd)

Neck and cuff ruffs

60 cm of 112 cm ($^3/_4$ yd of 44 in) wide pink satin

20 cm of 112 cm ($^1/_4$ yd of 44 in) wide yellow felt, or 2 squares, 30 x 30 cm (12 x 12 in)

1 cm ($^3/_8$ in) wide elastic: 1 m ($1^1/_8$ yd)

Hat

silver glitter clown hat

pink or yellow ribbon to fit around hat

1 scrap each of pink, yellow and green felt

scrap of pink nylon net (optional)

1.6 mm (14 gauge) galvanized tie wire: 10 cm (4 in)

Ready-made items

bright-coloured top

pink plastic boots

clown wig

red nose

How quick?

2 hrs

Time savers

Purchase braces

Purchase ready-made circle stickers

Little Helpers

This is an opportunity to let your child be really creative. In addition to the pink felt circles, your child could add other colourful shapes and decorative features, such as buttons, feathers and sequins, to both the trousers and the hat. Your little clown might also paint on his/her own clown features.

Ruffs

1 Cut one neck ruff 30 x 115 cm (12 x 45 in) and two cuff ruffs 15 x 115 cm (6 x 45 in) from pink satin. Using template on page 143, cut small circles from yellow felt and glue onto ruffs.

2 Stitch short ends of neck ruff together with right sides facing to form a ring. Press seam open. Repeat on cuff ruffs.

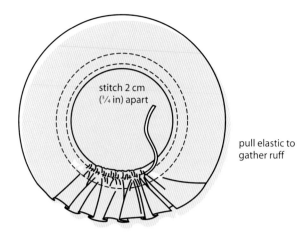

stitch 2 cm (³/₄ in) apart

pull elastic to gather ruff

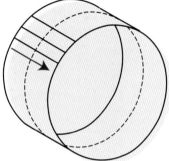

stitch short ends together and press seam open

4 On both neck and cuff ruffs, work a row of stitching 2 cm (³/₄ in) away from first row to form a casing. Thread elastic through casing and pull to create gathering. Tie a small double knot in elastic and push knot into casing. Hand-stitch hole closed.

3 Turn under seam allowance on raw edges and press. Fold neck ruff in half with wrong sides facing and pin pressed edges together. Topstitch pressed edges together, leaving a small opening for elastic. Repeat, using cuff ruffs.

Hat

1. Using the flower templates on page 143, cut one pink felt flower, one yellow felt flower centre and two green felt leaves. Also cut one green felt stem, 10 x 1 cm (4 x ³⁄₈ in). From pink net cut another flower (optional).

2. Place pink net flower (if used) over pink felt flower, and glue yellow centre on top. Allow to dry.

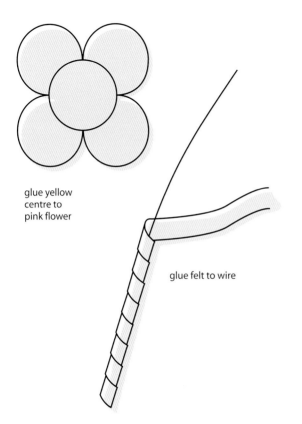

glue yellow
centre to
pink flower

glue felt to wire

3. Glue green felt around 10 cm (4 in) galvanized tie wire. Sew or glue leaves to top of stem, and glue flower on top.

4. Glue pink or yellow ribbon around base of hat and glue flower between ribbon and hat. Glue points of leaves to hat.

Complete the outfit

Finish with a bright-coloured top, plastic boots and clown wig. Paint on a clown face with face paints. Add red nose.

Buzzy bumble bee

With her bold black and gold stripes, net and marabou wings, and fetching feelers, this little bumble bee will create a buzz wherever she flies.

Equipment

sewing machine
sewing needle
scissors
pinking shears
black thread
pins
wire cutters
pliers
craft glue

Materials

Fur dress

2 m of 140 cm (2¼ yd of 55 in) wide black and gold fur fabric

12 mm (½ in) wide elastic: 1 m (1⅛ yd)

self-adhesive black Velcro: 20 cm (8 in)

Wings

60 cm of 112 cm (¾ yd of 44 in) wide black nylon net

black marabou trim, 2 m (2¼ yd)

1.6 mm diameter (14 gauge) galvanized tie wire: 1 m (1⅛ yd)

1 cm (⅜ in) wide black elastic: 1 m (1⅛ yd)

Hood and antennae

40 cm of 112 cm (½ yd of 44 in) wide black stretch velour fabric

black Alice band

2 fluffy black chenille sticks

2 black pompoms

self-adhesive black Velcro, 9 cm (3½ in)

Ready-made items

black leotard

black tights

black shoes (optional)

How quick?

2 hrs 45 mins

Time savers

Omit black velour hood, and use Alice band, with feelers, on its own.

Omit elastic gathering on dress.

Little helpers

Making small pompoms (see page 13) is a quick and easy task to keep your little bee busy.

To make
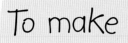

Trace Buzzy Bumble Bee patterns 11, 12 and 13 from pattern sheet, according to your child's age and height. Note that 1.5 cm (⅝ in) seam allowance has been included on all pattern pieces.

Fur dress

1 Fold fur fabric in half lengthways (across the stripes), with right sides together. Cut two dress pieces (pattern 12) on the fold, using pinking shears.

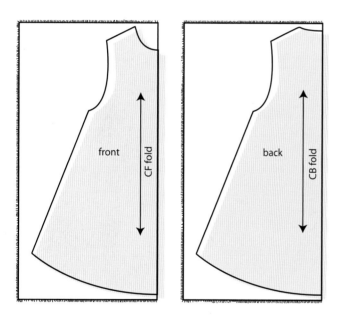

2 Place front and back panel pieces together with right sides facing, and stitch side seams. Turn up 2 cm (¾ in) along lower edge to make a casing, and stitch in place. Carefully cut a small hole in casing at one side seam. Thread elastic through casing. Tie a small double knot in elastic and thread knot into casing to conceal it. Note that more gathering can be achieved by using less elastic. Hand-stitch hole in casing to close it.

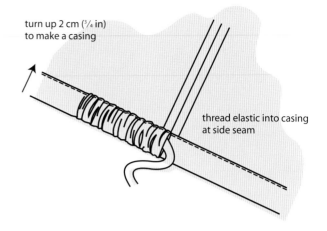

turn up 2 cm (¾ in) to make a casing

thread elastic into casing at side seam

3 Turn dress right side out. Stick 10 cm (4 in) of Velcro onto front and back of each shoulder so that the front shoulder will lie over back when fastened.

Wings

Using tie wire, net, marabou and elastic, make a pair of wings (see page 16).

Hood and antennae

1 With black velour fabric right side up, pin on hood (pattern 13) and cut one piece, using pinking shears. Cut another with fabric wrong side up, for a right and a left hood.

2 Zigzag-stitch around edges of fabric; this will prevent fraying and allow fabric stretch. Zigzag-stitch darts as indicated in illustration below.

3 Place two hood pieces together with right sides facing. Zigzag-stitch central seam. Then turn hood right side out, and stick one half of the Velcro on either side of the back opening.

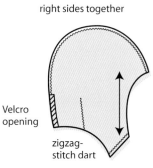

right sides together

Velcro opening

zigzag-stitch dart

4 Twist ends of chenille sticks around the Alice band to secure. Stitch black pompoms (see page 13) onto other ends of chenille sticks. Bend sticks to desired position.

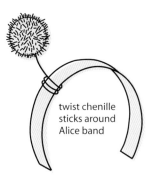

twist chenille sticks around Alice band

Complete the outfit

Team the costume with a black leotard, tights and shoes.

Floppy-eared rabbit

This cuddly, furry rabbit, with its perky pompom tail, will endear itself to one and all.
Complete the costume with a mask, a hood, or both.

Equipment

sewing machine

sewing needle

scissors

pinking shears

white and light brown thread

pins

craft glue

face paints (if not making mask)

Materials

Fur top

1.2 m of 140 cm (1³⁄₈ yd of 55 in) wide white fur fabric

80 cm of 140 cm (⁷⁄₈ yd of 55 in) wide light brown fur fabric

1 popper fastener

Mittens

20 cm of 140 cm (¹⁄₄ yd of 55 in) wide white fur fabric

piece of light brown felt, 20 x 30 cm (8 x 12 in)

piece of white felt, 20 x 10 cm (8 x 4 in)

Trousers

1.5 m of 140 cm (1³⁄₄ yd of 55 in) wide white fur fabric

2.5 cm (1 in) wide elastic: 50 cm (⁵⁄₈ yd)

Boots

40 cm of 140 cm (¹⁄₂ yd of 55 in) wide white fur fabric

piece of light brown felt, 30 x 30 cm (12 x 12 in)

piece of white felt, 20 x 10 cm (8 x 4 in)

Tail

white knitting yarn

small piece of cardboard

Mask (optional)

piece of lightweight card, 24 x 20 cm (9¹⁄₂ x 8 in)

piece of white fur fabric, 24 cm (in direction of pile) x 20 cm (9¹⁄₂ x 8 in)

scrap of light brown fur fabric

scrap each of light brown, black and white felt

shirring elastic: 30 cm (³⁄₈ yd)

Hood (optional)

50 cm of 140 cm (⁵⁄₈ in of 55 in) wide white fur fabric

30 cm of 140 cm (³⁄₈ yd of 55 in) wide light brown fur fabric

How quick?

2 hrs 40 mins

Time saver

Paint on a rabbit face with face paints.

To make

Trace Floppy-eared Rabbit template from page 141 and photocopy to enlarge to 100 per cent. Trace patterns 1, 2, 20, 37, 43, 44, 49, 50 and 51 from pattern sheet, according to your child's age and height. Note that 1.5 cm (⁵⁄₈ in) seam allowance has been included on all pattern pieces, apart from the mitten, which has a 1 cm (³⁄₈ in) seam allowance.

Fur top

Using white fur fabric for back and sleeves and light brown fur for front, make a basic tunic with back opening (see page 14). Neaten neckline by turning edge under and zigzag-stitching.

Mittens

1 Using white fur fabric and light brown felt, cut two mitten pieces (pattern 51) from each, reversing the pattern so you have a right and a left mitten piece in both fabrics. Make a pair of animal mittens (see page 17).

2 From white felt cut two of each pad piece, and glue to brown felt side of each mitten as indicated on pattern.

Trousers

Using white fur fabric, make a pair of basic trousers (see page 15).

Boots

1 Using white fur fabric for the uppers (pattern 49) and light brown felt for the soles (pattern 50), make a pair of animal boots (see page 16).

2 Cut two of each pad piece from white felt, and glue to sole of each boot as indicated on pattern.

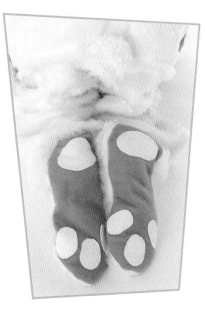

Tail

Make a large pompom in matching white yarn (see page 13), and stitch in place.

Mask (optional)

1 Using template on page 141, cut the following pieces: one head piece from lightweight card; one head piece from white fur fabric (with pile lengthways); a right and a left ear centre from light brown fur; a nose from light brown felt; teeth from white felt; a mouth piece from black felt; whisker strips from light brown felt.

2 Glue fur head piece to card head piece. Allow to dry. Glue on other features, and allow to dry.

3 Punch a hole on either side of mask. Thread shirring elastic through holes. Knot one end securely, try mask on child and adjust elastic for comfort. Knot remaining end and trim off any excess.

4 Try mask on child again and, using felt-tip pen, gently mark two dots for centres of eye holes. Remove mask. Using a coin of appropriate size as a template, draw eye holes; cut out.

Hood (optional)

Using white fur fabric for the crown, brim and outer ears and light brown fur fabric for the inner ears, as shown in photograph, make a rabbit hood (see page 17).

Complete the outfit

If not using a mask, paint on a rabbit face with face paints.

Faithful Dalmatian

This delightfully dotty Dalmatian is made in the same way as Floppy-eared Rabbit (page 80), but with a different fur and tail. Make a mask, a hood, or both.

Equipment

sewing machine

sewing needle

scissors

pinking shears

white and black thread

pins

craft glue

face paints (if not making mask)

Materials

Fur top

1.5 m of 140 cm (1³/₄ yd of 55 in) wide black and white fur fabric

6 cm (2¹/₂ in) wide red satin ribbon: 60 cm (³/₄ yd)

1 popper fastener

Mittens

20 cm of 140 cm (¹/₄ yd of 55 in) wide black and white fur fabric

piece of black felt, 20 x 30 cm (8 x 12 in)

piece of white felt, 20 x 10 cm (8 x 4 in)

Trousers

1.5 m of 140 cm (1³/₄ yd of 55 in) wide black and white fur fabric

2.5 cm (1 in) wide elastic, 50 cm (⁵/₈ yd)

Tail

piece of black and white fur fabric, 38 cm (lengthways grain) x 12 cm (15 x 5 in)

piece of thin polyester wadding, 38 x 12 cm (15 x 5 in)

1.6 mm (14 gauge) galvanized tie wire: 30 cm (12 in)

Boots

40 cm of 140 cm (¹/₂ yd of 55 in) wide black and white fur fabric

piece of black felt, 30 x 30 cm (12 x 12 in)

piece of white felt, 20 x 10 cm (8 x 4 in)

Mask (optional)

piece of lightweight card, 28 x 18 cm (11 x 7 in)

piece of black and white fur fabric, 16 cm (direction of pile) x 20 cm (6¹/₂ x 8 in)

piece of black fur fabric, 18 cm (direction of pile) x 25 cm (7 x 10 in)

scraps of pink and black felt

shirring elastic: 30 cm (³/₈ yd)

Hood (optional)

50 cm of 140 cm (⁵/₈ yd of 55 in) wide black and white fur fabric

30 cm of 140 cm (³/₈ yd of 55 in) wide black fur fabric

Collar tag

piece of silver card, 6 x 6 cm (2¹/₂ x 2¹/₂ in)

How quick?

2 hrs 40 mins

Time saver

For mask, simply draw or paint features onto white card.

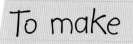

To make

Trace Faithful Dalmatian templates from pages 141–2 and photocopy to enlarge to 100 per cent. Trace patterns 1, 2, 20, 37, 43, 44, 49, 50 and 51 from pattern sheet, according to your child's age and height. Note that 1.5 cm (⅝ in) seam allowance has been included on all pattern pieces, apart from the mitten, which has a 1 cm (⅜ in) seam allowance.

Fur top

From black and white fur fabric make a basic tunic with back opening (see page 14). Use red satin ribbon to bind neck edge.

Mittens

1 Using black and white fur fabric and black felt, cut two mitten pieces (pattern 51) from each, reversing the pattern so that you have a right and a left mitten piece in both fabrics. Make a pair of animal mittens (see page 17).

2 From white felt, cut two of each pad piece and glue them to felt side of mittens as indicated on pattern.

Trousers

Using black and white fur fabric, make a pair of basic trousers (see page 15).

Tail

1 Fold piece of black and white fur fabric in half lengthways, with wrong sides facing. Pin tail pattern on fold, with fur pile sloping from wider to narrower end of pattern. Cut another piece from wadding.

2 Re-fold fur tail with right sides facing. Machine-stitch long sides and smaller end together. Trim seam allowance to 5 mm (¼ in) and turn tail right side out.

3 Cover the wire with wadding and glue wadding edges together. Pull fur tail over wadding. Trim wadding slightly, fold in fur edges, and slipstitch together. Add a safety pin at wider end for attaching tail to costume. Bend tail into desired position.

Boots

Using black and white fur fabric for the uppers (pattern 49), and combining black felt and white felt for the soles (pattern 50), make a pair of animal boots (see page 16).

Mask (optional)

1 Using template on page 141, cut the following: one head piece from lightweight card; one face piece from black and white fur fabric (with pile lengthways); a right and left ear from black fur fabric; a tongue from pink felt; a nose, a mouth piece and four whiskers from black felt.

2 Glue face and ear pieces to card head piece. Allow to dry. Glue on other features, and allow to dry.

3 Punch a hole on either side of mask. Thread shirring elastic through holes. Knot one end securely, try mask on child and adjust elastic for comfort. Knot remaining end and trim off any excess.

4 Try mask on child again and, using felt-tip pen, gently mark two dots for centres of eye holes. Remove mask. Using a coin of appropriate size as a template, draw eye holes; cut out eye holes.

Hood (optional)

Using black and white fur fabric for the crown and brim and black fur fabric for the ears, as shown in photograph, make a Dalmatian hood (see page 17).

Collar tag

Using the template on page 142, cut a small circle from silver card and glue to red satin ribbon. Your child might like his/her name, or the name of a real dog, written on the tag.

Complete the outfit

If not using a mask, paint on a doggy face with face paints.

To make

Trace template from page 141 and photocopy to enlarge to 100 per cent. Trace patterns 1, 2, 20, 37, 40, 42, 44, 49, 50 and 51 from pattern sheet, according to child's age and height. A 1.5 cm (⅝ in) seam allowance has been included on all pattern pieces, apart from the mitten, which has a 1 cm (⅜ in) seam allowance.

Fur top

1 Using light brown or dark brown fur fabric, make a basic tunic with back opening (see page 14). Neaten the neck edges by turning under and zigzag-stitching.

2 **Teddy Bear** To make tummy look padded, turn up 3 cm (1¼ in) on hem edge to make a casing. Stitch close to raw edge. Carefully cut a small hole in casing at side seam. Thread elastic through casing. Overlap ends of elastic and stitch together by hand or machine. More gathering can be achieved by using less elastic. Hand-stitch hole to close.

3 **Teddy Bear** Zigzag-stitch spotted red fabric patch, 10 x 10 cm (4 x 4 in). Using thick brown thread, add a few straight stitches over the edge of the patch for additional decoration.

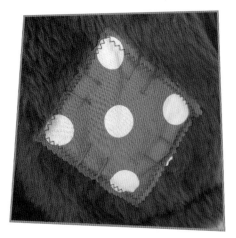

Mittens

1 Using brown fur fabric and felt in appropriate shades, cut two mitten pieces (pattern 51) from each, reversing the pattern so you have a right and a left mitten piece in both fabrics and making sure pile runs lengthways. Make a pair of animal mittens (see page 17).

2 From contrasting felt, cut two of each pad piece and glue to felt side of each mitten as indicated on pattern.

Trousers

1 Using light brown or dark brown fur fabric, make a pair of basic trousers (see page 15).

2 **Teddy Bear** Using zigzag stitch and adding straight stitches, as for fur top, add a patch of red spotted fabric, 10 x 10 cm (4 x 4 in) to trouser leg in desired position.

3 Using brown knitting yarn, make a large pompom (see page 13). Sew to trousers.

Boots

Using light brown (Teddy) or dark brown (Big Bear) fur fabric for the uppers (pattern 49), and contrasting dark brown and light brown felt for the soles and paw pads (pattern 50), make a pair of animal boots (see page 16).

Teddy Bear's bow tie

1 From red spotted fabric, cut a main bow tie piece 40 x 24 cm (15^1/$_2$ x 9^1/$_2$ in) and a centre bow tie piece 24 x 10 cm (9^1/$_2$ x 4 in), using pinking shears.

2 Fold main section in half lengthways, with right sides facing, and stitch two edges together, leaving one end open. Turn right side out. Slip piece of wadding through open end. Turn in raw edges and slipstitch them together neatly.

3 Press under both long edges of centre tie by 3 cm (1^1/$_4$ in). Pull centre around middle of main section to form a bow shape. Stitch or glue ends of centre tie together at back of bow.

4 Stitch bow tie to front of Teddy Bear neck.

Mask (optional)

1 Using template on page 141, cut the following: one head piece from lightweight card; one head piece from light brown (Teddy)/dark brown fur fabric (with pile vertical); two ear centres from dark brown (Teddy)/light brown fur fabric; a muzzle from dark brown (Teddy)/light brown fur; a nose from light brown (Teddy)/black felt; a mouth piece from black felt.

2 Glue fur head piece to card head piece. Allow to dry. Glue on other features, and allow to dry.

3 Punch a hole on either side of mask. Thread shirring elastic through holes. Knot one end securely, try mask on child and adjust elastic for comfort. Knot remaining end and trim off any excess.

4 Try mask on child again and, using felt-tip pen, gently mark two dots for centres of eye holes. Remove mask. Using a coin as a template, draw eye holes. Cut out eye holes.

Hood (optional)

Using light and dark brown fur as shown in photographs, make a bear hood (see page 17).

Complete the outfit

If not using a mask, paint on bear features with face paints.

Pirate

You can improvise a pirate costume from a striped T-shirt, a bandanna and an eye patch. Or follow these instructions, using materials from your own treasure trove.

Equipment

sewing machine

sewing needle

scissors

pinking shears

small, sharp-pointed scissors

black and red thread

pins

craft glue

dressmaker's carbon paper

Materials

Waistcoat

1.2 m of 112 cm ($1^3/8$ yd of 44 in) wide black cotton drill

scrap of white felt, 8 x 8 cm (3 x 3 in)

Trousers

1.5 m of 112 cm ($1^3/4$ yd of 44 in) wide black cotton drill

20 cm of 112 cm ($1/4$ yd of 44 in) wide red cotton poplin

2.5 cm (1 in) wide elastic: 50 cm ($5/8$ yd)

Cummerbund

50 cm of 112 cm ($5/8$ yd of 44 in) wide red cotton poplin

Bandanna

50 cm of 112 cm ($5/8$ yd of 44 in) wide red cotton poplin

scrap of black cotton drill

Eye patch

piece of black felt, 8 x 8 cm (3 x 3 in)

piece of lightweight cardboard, 8 x 8 cm (3 x 3 in)

black shirring elastic: approximately 30 cm (12 in)

Ready-made items

striped top

pirate accessories

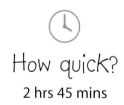

How quick?

2 hrs 45 mins

Time savers

Instead of making trousers, cut an old pair into long shorts with pinking shears. Glue on knee patches.

Omit waistcoat and wear striped T-shirt with a belt and plastic skull accessory.

Little helpers

Designing a T-shirt is an easy task to keep your little pirate amused. Simply paint stripes as desired on an old T-shirt or long-sleeved top, using fabric paint. Trim the sleeves and lower edge with pinking shears for a rough effect. Your child may also enjoy using face paints to create a moustache, beard and gruesome scars.

To make

Trace Pirate templates from page 142 and photocopy to enlarge to 100 per cent. Trace patterns 20, 21 and 29 from pattern sheet, according to your child's age. Note that 1.5 cm ($^5/_8$ in) seam allowance has been included, where appropriate, on all pattern pieces.

Waistcoat

1 Using black cotton drill, make a basic waistcoat (see page 15), omitting the ties.

2 Trace and enlarge the skull and crossbones motif on page 142 and use dressmaker's carbon paper to transfer it to the scrap of white felt. Cut out motif with sharp-pointed scissors. Stitch or glue it onto front of waistcoat in desired position.

Trousers

1 From black cotton drill, cut out pieces for a pair of basic trousers (see page 15).

2 Before joining trouser pieces, use pinking shears to cut two trouser patches, each 28 x 15 cm (11 x 6 in), from double thickness red cotton poplin, with short edge against the fold. Zigzag-stitch patches onto trousers as shown in photograph.

Cummerbund

1 Cut two pieces of red cotton poplin, 100 x 25 cm (40 x 10 in), using pinking shears.

2 Place fabric pieces next to each other, overlapping the ends by 2 cm ($^3/_4$ in). Zigzag-stitch overlapped edges together, then zigzag-stitch around all edges to decorate. In dressing child, place seam at centre front and tie ends at back.

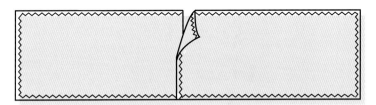

overlap ends by 2 cm ($^3/_4$ in)

Bandanna

1 With red poplin folded double, pin on bandanna piece (pattern 29) and cut, using pinking shears to prevent the edges fraying.

2 Zigzag-stitch around edges with black thread to decorate.

3 Cut one bandanna patch, about 9 x 9 cm ($3^{1}/_{2}$ x $3^{1}/_{2}$ in), from black drill. Zigzag-stitch onto bandanna at widest part, as shown in photograph, using red thread.

thread elastic through holes

Eye patch

1 Using the template on page 142, cut one eye patch piece from black felt and one from card. Glue the felt to the card patch.

2 Punch a hole at either side of patch and thread through enough shirring elastic to fit around head. Tie ends of elastic together in a knot.

Complete the outfit

Finish the costume by teaming it with child's own striped top. Pirate accessories, such as a parrot, treasure chest, sword and pistol, can be purchased.

Native Americans

Creating a Native American costume for a boy or girl is easy, using basic tunic and trouser patterns. You can then embellish them with your choice of craft accessories.

Equipment

- sewing machine
- sewing needle
- scissors
- pinking shears
- beige and black thread
- pins
- craft glue
- hole punch
- liquid fray preventer
- fabric paints
- face paints

Materials

Boy

Tunic

1.5 m of 112 cm (1³/₄ yd of 44 in) wide unbleached calico

50 cm of 112 cm (⁵/₈ yd of 44 in) wide brown imitation suede fabric

50 cm of 112 cm (⁵/₈ yd of 44 in) wide red cotton

1 cm (³/₈ in) wide red bias binding: 40 cm (¹/₂ yd)

selection of craft accessories, such as beads, ethnic braid, feathers

1 popper fastener

Trousers

1.5 m of 112 cm (1³/₄ yd of 44 in) wide unbleached calico

50 cm of 112 cm (⁵/₈ yd of 44 in) wide red cotton fabric

2.5 cm (1 in) wide elastic: 50 cm (⁵/₈ yd)

2 cm (³/₄ in) wide ethnic braid: 1 m (1¹/₈ yd)

red feathers (optional)

Headdress

5 cm (2 in) wide ethnic braid: 80 cm (⁷/₈ yd)

small strip of felt, any colour

one or more feathers

Tomahawk

piece of silver card, approximately 12 x 8 cm (5 x 4 in) (or twice this size if white on one side)

twig or narrow bamboo stick

thin leather thong: 1 m (1¹/₈ yd)

scrap of suede tassel fabric

Girl

Tunic

1.5 m of 112 cm (1³/₄ yd of 44 in) wide unbleached calico

50 cm of 112 cm (⁵/₈ yd of 44 in) wide brown imitation suede fabric

50 cm of 112 cm (⁵/₈ yd of 44 in) wide red cotton

piece of red felt, approximately 8 x 8 cm (3 x 3 in)

1 cm (³/₈ in) wide red bias binding: 60 cm (³/₄ yd)

thin leather thong: 50 cm (⁵/₈ yd)

selection of craft accessories, such as beads, ethnic braid, feathers

1 popper fastener

Trousers

1.5 m of 112 cm (1³/₄ yd of 44 in) wide unbleached calico

50 cm of 112 cm (⁵/₈ yd of 44 in) wide red cotton fabric

piece of brown imitation suede fabric, 25 x 8 cm (10 x 3 in)

2.5 cm (1 in) wide elastic: 50 cm (⁵/₈ yd)

Headdress

5 cm (2 in) wide ethnic braid: 80 cm (⁷/₈ yd)

small strip of felt, any colour

one or more feathers

How quick?

2 hrs each costume

Time savers

Glue rather than stitch braid onto costumes, or simply paint patterns directly onto fabric using fabric paint.

Purchase headdress and tomahawk from specialist fancy-dress shop.

Little helpers

Children will enjoy using fabric paints to colour the tips of feathers and create ethnic patterns on the costumes.

To make

Trace Native American templates from page 143 and photocopy to enlarge to 100 per cent. Trace patterns 1, 2, 20, 45 and 46 from pattern sheet, according to your child's age and height. Note that 1.5 cm ($^5/_8$ in) seam allowance has been included on pattern pieces where appropriate. The construction method is almost the same for both costumes; any differences are stated within the basic instructions.

Tunic

1 Using unbleached calico, cut pieces for a basic tunic with back opening (see page 14). **Girl** Using pinking shears, cut 10 cm (4 in) into centre front neck edge to form a V shape. Cut notched fringe on sleeves and lower hem as indicated.

2 Before joining seams, decorate front and back tunic pieces, using photographs as a guide. For fringe, cut one piece of brown suede fabric 62 x 8 cm (24$^1/_2$ x 3 in) and two pieces 32 x 8 cm (12$^1/_2$ x 3 in). Cut into fabric to make fringe. For belt, cut one piece 62 x 4 cm (24$^1/_2$ x 1$^1/_2$ in) and two pieces 32 x 4 cm (12$^1/_2$ x 1$^1/_2$ in). Stitch belt and fringe pieces to tunic front and backs.

3 **Boy** From brown suede cut two zigzag sleeve details (pattern 45) and two sleeve edge bands (50 x 5 cm/20 x 2 in); also one neck detail square (using template on page 143). From red fabric cut two notched sleeve details (pattern 46), one neck detail (using template on page 143) and one belt flap, 12 x 14 cm (5 x 5$^1/_2$ in). **Girl** From red fabric cut a strip 62 x 4 cm (24$^1/_2$ x 1$^1/_2$ in) and two strips 32 x 4 cm (12$^1/_2$ x 1$^1/_2$ in). Zigzag-stitch details on front and back tunic pieces as shown in photographs. Alternatively, paint or glue on decoration.

4 **Girl** Zigzag-stitch raw edges of front neck opening or apply liquid fray preventer. From red felt cut eight squares, each 2 x 2 cm ($^3/_4$ x $^3/_4$ in), and glue around neckline. Punch two holes on either side of neck opening.

5 Join the tunic seams. Bind neck edges with red bias binding. **Girl** Thread leather thong through holes; if desired, knot a couple of small beads onto the end of each thong.

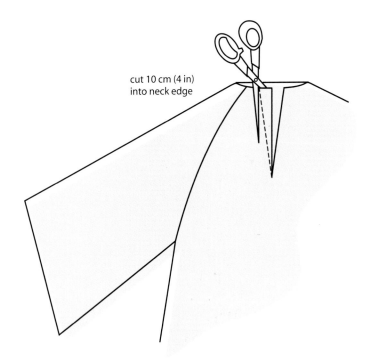

cut 10 cm (4 in) into neck edge

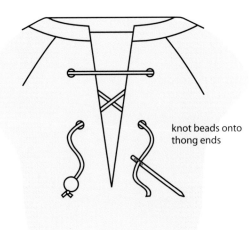

knot beads onto thong ends

Trousers

1 Using unbleached calico, cut out pieces for basic trousers (see page 15). **Boy** Using pinking shears, cut notched fringe around legs as indicated on pattern piece.

2 Before joining seams, decorate trousers. **Boy** From red fabric cut two strips, 50 x 8 cm (20 x 3 in), using pinking shears. Zigzag-stitch to trousers where shown in photograph. **Girl** From red fabric cut two strips 50 x 3 cm (20 x 1¼ in), using pinking shears. Cut brown suede fabric into two strips, 25 x 3 cm (10 x 1¼ in), using pinking shears. Zigzag-stitch red band to trousers. Add a large zigzag line of straight stitching on top of band, if desired.

3 Make up the trousers as instructed on page 15. **Boy** Stitch a few feathers, if desired, to each red band, as shown in photograph. **Girl** Tie brown suede fabric in a knot and hand-stitch to each red band.

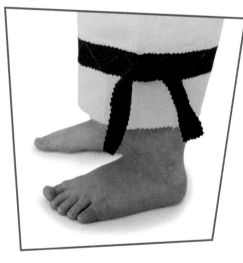

Tomahawk

Using the template on page 143, cut one tomahawk piece from silver card. (If card is not silver on both sides, cut two and glue together.) Punch two holes close to straight edge. Thread twig through holes, and wind leather thong around twig to hold 'blade' in place. Tie suede tassel onto end of thong.

Complete the outfit

Plait hair and use face paints to make bold face stripes.

Headdress

Glue painted feather(s) to inside of ethnic braid. Once dry, glue a small piece of felt over ends of the feathers for comfort. Tie braid around head and secure in knot at the back.

High-tech robot

Don't be fooled by all the gadgetry! This state-of-the-art robot costume is very simple and inexpensive to make.

Equipment

sewing machine

sewing needle

scissors

pinking shears

silver thread

pins

craft glue

stapler

silver spray paint

Materials

Silver tunic

1.5 m of 112 cm (1³/₄ yd of 44 in) wide silver polyester foil fabric

1 popper fastener

Trousers

1.5 m of 112 cm (1³/₄ yd of 44 in) wide silver polyester foil fabric

2.5 cm (1 in) wide elastic: 50 cm (⁵/₈ yd)

Silver body box

large cardboard box

a selection of silver card, craft balls, black felt, silver polyester foil fabric, black chenille sticks

bubble wrap (optional)

Silver head box

small cardboard box

small piece of black net

silver pipe lagging: 1m (1¹/₈ yd)

selection of craft balls and black and red chenille sticks

bubble wrap (optional)

Ready-made items

Plastic boots

How quick?

2 hrs 45 mins

Time savers

Simply paint control features onto the front of the box.

Use grey marl tracksuit instead of making tunic and trousers.

Little helpers

This is an opportunity for your child to be as creative as he desires. Let the control panel be his own project, and he can spend hours cutting, sticking and painting shapes as he wishes.

To make

Trace High-tech Robot patterns 1, 2, 20, 31, 32 and 33 from pattern sheet, according to your child's age. Note that 1.5 cm ($^5/_8$ in) seam allowance has been included on all pattern pieces.

If the boxes have any lettering or other areas that should be concealed, glue pieces of bubble wrap over these. Spray entire cardboard boxes, including bubble wrap, with silver spray paint.

Silver tunic top

Using silver polyester foil fabric, make a basic tunic with back opening (see page 14). Neaten the neck edge by turning under and zigzag-stitching.

Trousers

Using silver polyester foil fabric, make a pair of basic trousers (see page 15).

Silver head and body boxes

1 Turn small box so that the opening is towards you. Using the head pattern piece (pattern 31) as a guide – and amending pattern, if necessary, to suit child's face – mark and cut out eye and mouth holes with a pair of scissors.

2 Glue a piece of black net behind each eye hole. Glue a chenille stick around eye and mouth openings to create a neat edge.

glue black net behind eye holes

glue chenille sticks around eye and mouth holes

3 Turn silver body box so that the opening is facing downwards. Place head box, centred, on top, with all lid flaps turned under. Holding the head box firmly in place, draw a line along its side edges. Remove head box. With a pair of scissors, cut through the pencil lines to create slits. Replace head box and mark its front and back edges. Find the centre point between marked lines and slits, and mark it on body box.

4 Measure width of child's head, generously, and mark half this measurement to either side of centre point. Cut a rectangular hole to this width by the full distance between marked front and back lines. Make sure that child's head will go through hole comfortably. Trim back and front flaps so they will fit in hole. Feed side flaps through slits, and fix to underside of body box with glue or staples.

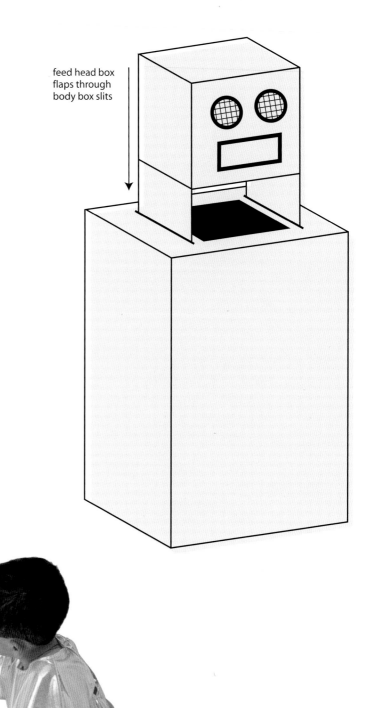

feed head box flaps through body box slits

5 Cut a hole near the top of both sides of the body box for arm access. Cut holes to accommodate pipe lagging on both sides of the head box and shoulders, and insert lagging.

6 Using the photograph and panel detail pattern pieces (patterns 32 and 33) as guides, cut out silver card and felt decorations and attach to the front control panel. Insert silver-sprayed chenille sticks with craft balls on the end to suggest levers on the control panel and antennae.

Complete the outfit

Spray a pair of old plastic boots with silver spray paint and leave to dry.

insert pipe lagging

Airy fairy

Any little Tinker Bell would love this enchanting costume. The soft pink net, shimmering satin and twinkling stars are just dazzling.

Equipment

sewing machine

sewing needle

scissors

pinking shears

pink thread

pins

craft glue

Materials

Dress

1.5 m of 112 cm (1³/₄ yd of 44 in) wide pink satin lining fabric

1.5 m of 112 cm (1³/₄ yd of 44 in) wide pink net

3 cm (1¹/₄ in) wide pink ribbon: 3 m (3³/₈ yd)

3 popper fasteners

Wings

60 cm of 112 cm (³/₄ yd of 44 in) wide pink nylon net

pink marabou trim: 2 m (2¹/₄ yd)

1.6 mm diameter (14 gauge) galvanized tie wire: 1 m (1¹/₈ yd)

1 cm (³/₈ in) wide pink elastic: 1 m (1¹/₈ yd)

sheet of pink foil for stars

Ready-made items

tiara

fairy wand

How quick?

3 hrs

Time savers

Buy pink stick-on stars.

Use purchased wings.

To make

Trace Airy Fairy template from page 143 and photocopy to enlarge to 100 per cent. Trace patterns 3, 4, 6 and 11 from pattern sheet, according to child's age. Note that 1.5 cm (⅝ in) seam allowance has been included on all pattern pieces.

Dress

1 Fold pink net in half lengthways, pin bodice (pattern 3) on fold, and cut out as indicated for bodice front, using pinking shears. With fabric still double, pin on bodice pattern and cut two bodice back pieces. Fold pink satin in half lengthways, with right sides facing, and cut out same pieces as for the net.

2 With pink net double, pin on skirt (pattern 6) and cut out as indicated for two skirts and two top skirts. With net double, cut two sleeves (pattern 4). Cut one more skirt from a single layer of net, for three skirt pieces. Cut same pieces from pink satin.

3 With right sides together, stitch satin front bodice to satin back bodice at shoulder and side seams, leaving centre back seam open. Press seam allowances open and turn bodice right side out. Repeat using net.

4 With right sides facing, stitch satin bodice and net bodice together around neck opening and centre back edges. Turn bodice right side out. Turn under a small hem on armholes and stitch. Stitch 3 poppers in place down centre back edges as indicated on pattern piece.

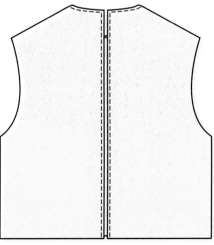

stitch satin and net bodices together at neck and centre back edges

stitch armhole hem

5 With right sides together stitch net sleeve to satin sleeve, leaving an opening of approximately 15 cm (6 in). Turn right side out. Slipstitch opening edges to close. Topstitch or glue sleeves to top edge of armholes.

6 Place a pink net skirt piece over each pink satin skirt piece, with right side of satin upwards. Pin the three sections together at side edges, with net and satin layers together, and zigzag-stitch four seams as shown in illustration. Repeat with the two top skirt net and satin sections.

zigzag-stitch net and satin pieces at side edges

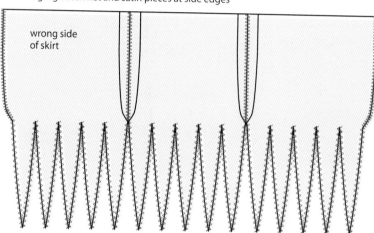

wrong side of skirt

7 Using the longest machine stitch, work two lines of stitching, 1 cm (³⁄₈ in) apart across the top edge of skirt and top skirt. Pull both bobbin threads to gather each skirt to fit bodice. Knot thread ends to secure them, and adjust gathers evenly.

8 With right sides together, stitch skirt to lower edge of bodice. Turn dress right side out.

9 Stitch one edge of pink ribbon over gathered edge of top skirt. Tie ribbon around waist of dress, and secure in a bow at the back.

Wings

1 Using pink net, marabou and tie wire, make a pair of wings (see page 16). Attach elastic for arms.

2 Using template on page 143, cut stars from pink foil and glue to pink net on wings.

Complete the outfit

As a finishing touch, add a tiara and a fairy wand.

Fluttery butterfly

This colourful costume is as simple to make as it is fun to wear – a great idea for a last-minute invitation to a fancy-dress party.

Equipment

- sewing needle
- scissors
- black thread
- pins
- craft glue

Materials

Wings

2 m of 112 cm (2¼ yd of 44 in) wide black felt

1.5 m of 112 cm (1¾ yd of 44 in) wide red felt

40 cm of 112 cm (³/₈ yd of 44 in) wide yellow felt, or 4 squares, 30 x 30 cm (12 x 12 in)

1 cm (³/₈ in) wide black elastic: 1.5 m (1¾ yd)

Feelers

black velvet Alice band

2 red pipe cleaners, 25 cm (10 in) long

Ready-made items

black leotard

black tights

black shoes (optional)

How quick?
1 hr

Little helpers

Your little butterfly might enjoy gluing the spots onto the wings.

To make

Trace Fluttery Butterfly patterns 14, 15, 16, 17, 18 and 19 from pattern sheet.

Wings

1 Fold black felt in half widthways. Pin large wing piece (pattern 14) on the fold and cut out.

2 From red felt cut eight each of stripe A (pattern 15) and stripe B (pattern 16). Cut four of stripe C (pattern 17).

3 Glue red felt pieces onto black wings as indicated on pattern and in the illustration (right).

4 From yellow felt cut twenty of larger spot B (pattern 19). Glue onto wings as indicated on pattern and in the illustration.

5 From black felt cut twelve of smaller spot A (pattern 18). Glue onto wings as indicated on pattern and in the illustration.

6 Turn wings over and glue on decorations as before.

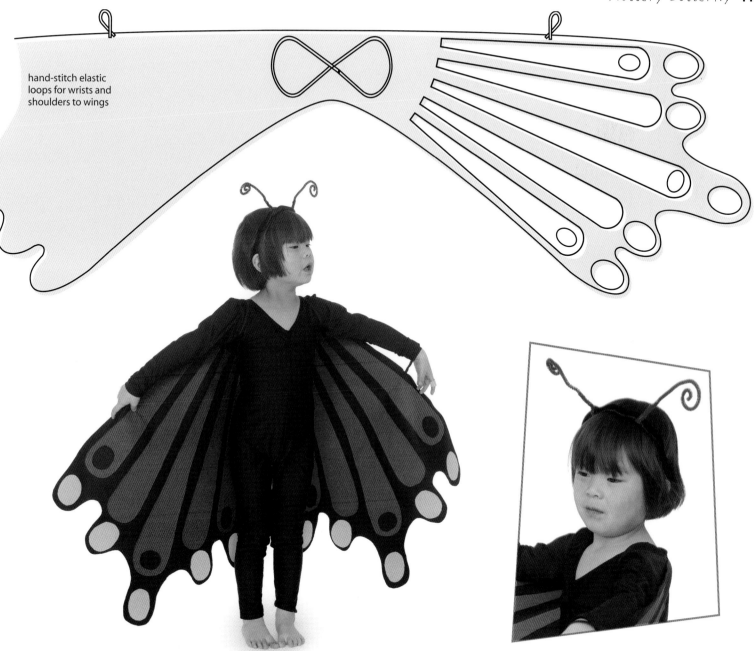

hand-stitch elastic loops for wrists and shoulders to wings

7 Make even loops of elastic to slip over each shoulder, and hand-stitch to centre of one side of wings. Make even loops of elastic to fit around wrists, and hand-stitch to wing as indicated on pattern piece and illustration.

Feelers

Wrap one end of each pipe cleaner around Alice band. Curl other end as shown in the photograph.

Complete the outfit

Set the wings off with a black leotard and tights.

Cheeky Elf

This easy-to-make costume is just the thing for your little imp to wear while getting up to mischief!

Equipment

sewing machine

sewing needle

scissors

pinking shears

green and beige thread

pins

craft glue

Materials

Tabard

80 cm of 112 cm (³/₄ yd of 44 in) wide green felt

20 cm of 112 cm (¹/₄ yd of 44 in) wide beige felt

2 cm (³/₄ in) wide self-adhesive beige Velcro: 10 cm (¹/₈ yd)

2 green buttons

1 popper fastener

Hat

30 cm of 112 cm (³/₈ yd of 44 in) wide beige felt

Boots

40 cm of 112 cm (¹/₂ yd of 44 in) wide green felt

Ready-made items

long-sleeved beige top

beige tights

How quick?

1 hr 45 mins

Time savers

Omit boots.
Omit collar piece.

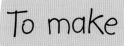

To make

Trace Cheeky Elf patterns 8, 9, 10, 47 and 48 from pattern sheet, according to your child's age. Note that 1.5 cm ($^5/_8$ in) seam allowance has been included on all pattern pieces, apart from the hat, which has 1 cm ($^3/_8$ in) seam allowance.

Tabard

1 Fold green felt double, pin tabard piece (pattern 8) onto fabric fold and cut tabard front. Repeat, for an identical back piece. For belt cut one strip of beige felt 58 x 4.5 cm (23 x 1$^3/_4$ in) and one strip 34 x 4.5 cm (13$^1/_2$ x 1$^3/_4$ in). Also from beige felt, cut the collar piece (pattern 10), on the fold.

2 Join front to back at shoulder seams.

3 Stitch longer (back) belt to one side of tabard where indicated on pattern piece, making sure that excess length at the two edges is equal. Stitch front belt to tabard where indicated on pattern piece.

4 Cut the Velcro into two pieces, and stick one half of each piece to one end of a front and back belt where the back belt overlaps the front.

5 Hand-stitch a decorative green button to each end of back belt as shown in the photograph.

6 Stitch popper to collar where indicated on pattern piece.

Hat

1 From beige felt, cut six hat pieces (pattern 9).

2 Join hat pieces at side edges, taking 1 cm (³/₈ in) seam allowance. Turn hat right side out.

join at
side edges

press open seam
allowance on
wrong side

Boots

Using green felt, make a pair of basic boots (see page 16).

Complete the outfit

Add a beige or brown long-sleeved top and tights/leggings.

Handsome prince

Clad in satin, adorned with gold and fur trimmings and sparkling gems, and wearing a gold crown, this elegant young man awaits his princess.

Equipment

sewing machine

sewing needle

scissors

pinking shears

gold, yellow and purple thread

pins

craft glue

Materials

Cape

2.5 m of 112 cm (2³/₄ yd of 44 in) wide purple satin

50 cm of 112 cm (⁵/₈ yd of 44 in) wide black and white fur fabric

4 cm (1¹/₂ in) wide gold ribbon: 40 cm (¹/₂ yd)

fake gemstones or sequins

1 popper fastener

Tunic

2.5 m of 112 cm (2³/₄ yd of 44 in) wide yellow satin

2.5 cm (1 in) wide gold ribbon: 4 m (4¹/₂ yd)

fake gemstones

1 popper fastener

Boots

40 cm of 112 cm (¹/₂ yd of 44 in) wide purple satin or felt

Crown

sheet of silver or gold card, at least 57 x 16 cm (22¹/₂ x 6¹/₂ in)

3 cm (1¹/₄ in) wide strip of black and white fur fabric: 57 cm (22¹/₂ in)

fake gemstones and/or sequins

How quick?

2 hrs 45 mins

Time saver

Use purchased crown.

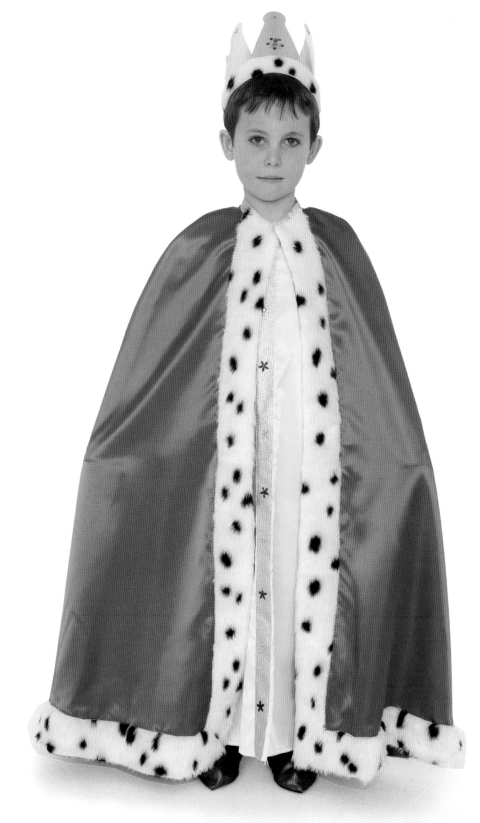

To make

Trace Handsome Prince patterns 1, 2, 22, 23, 24, 36, 47 and 48 from pattern sheet, according to child's age. Note that 1.5 cm ($^5/_8$ in) seam allowance has been included on all pattern pieces.

Cape

1 Fold purple satin in half lengthways, right sides facing. Pin cape (pattern 22) on the fold and cut out as indicated for cape back, using pinking shears. From remaining purple satin, cut two cape front pieces, not on the fold, so you have a right and a left front. From fur fabric, cut two front trim pieces (pattern 23). Cut three hem trim pieces (pattern 24), cutting one on the fold.

2 With right sides together, stitch satin fronts to satin back at side edges. Press seams open. Snip into curved edges to allow fabric to lie flat.

3 Turn under a narrow hem on side and bottom edges of cape, and stitch in place.

4 Bind neck edge with gold ribbon.

5 Stitch strips of fur fabric together as indicated on pattern pieces. Glue fur trim to front edges and hem of cape.

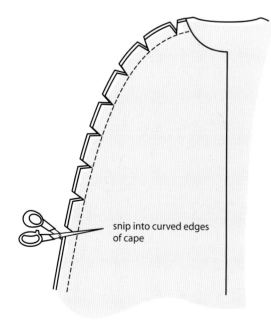

snip into curved edges of cape

Tunic

1 Using yellow satin, make a basic tunic with back opening (see page 14). Bind neckline with gold ribbon.

2 Glue or stitch gold ribbon down centre front of tunic, and glue on fake gems to decorate, as shown in the photograph.

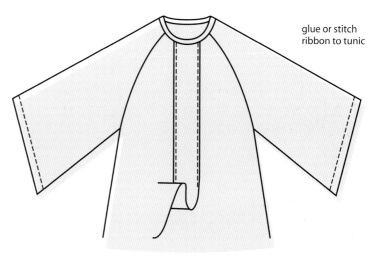

glue or stitch ribbon to tunic

Boots

Using purple fabric, make a pair of basic boots (see page 16).

Crown

1 Cut crown (pattern 36) from gold or silver card.

2 Overlap edges and glue together. Glue fur around lower edge of crown and glue on fake gems or sequins as shown in the photograph.

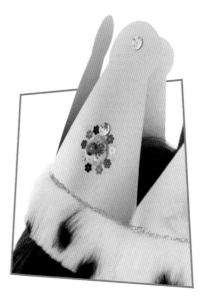

Beautiful princess

In this glamorous dress, made of sequin-trimmed satin and organza, and wearing a tiara, your little princess will certainly sparkle.

Equipment

sewing machine
sewing needle
scissors
pinking shears
purple thread
pins
craft glue

Materials

Dress

2.5 m of 112 cm (2³⁄₄ yd of 44 in) wide purple satin

1 m of 112 cm (1¹⁄₈ yd of 44 in) wide purple organza

2 m of 112 cm (2¹⁄₄ yd of 44 in) wide white net

1 cm (³⁄₈ in) wide flexible lightweight boning: 1.2m (1³⁄₈ yd)

3 cm (1¹⁄₄ in) wide purple ribbon: 3 m (3³⁄₈ yd)

strip of silver sequins: 50 cm (⁵⁄₈ yd)

3 popper fasteners

Ready-made items

tiara
white tights
dressy shoes

How quick?

4 hrs

Time savers

Omit the sequins and organza inset on bodice.

Omit the top skirt.

Omit the white net petticoat.

To make

Trace Beautiful Princess patterns 3, 5 and 7 from pattern sheet, according to your child's age. Note that 1.5 cm ($^5/_8$ in) seam allowance has been included on all pattern pieces.

Cutting out

1 Fold purple satin in half lengthways with right sides facing. Pin skirt (pattern 7) on fold and cut out using pinking shears. Repeat to cut another skirt piece. Cut out two pieces of satin facing for petticoat hem (as indicated on pattern 7). Cut out two more skirt pieces from white net.

2 With purple satin still folded, pin bodice (pattern 3) on the fold and cut out a front bodice, using pinking shears. Repeat to cut another front bodice piece. From remaining purple satin, cut four back bodice pieces, not on the fold, so that you have two right and two left back bodice pieces.

3 From double thickness purple organza, cut two top skirt pieces (as indicated on pattern 7) on the fold, using pinking shears. Also from organza, cut one bodice inset (as shown in photograph) and two sleeve pieces (pattern 5).

Bodice

1 Pin and tack organza inset to one front bodice piece. Stitch in place, close to the edge. Using the widest and longest zigzag stitch, sew a sequin strip to both side edges of organza; fasten the stitching within the armhole and waistline seam allowances, but do not extend the sequins into the seam allowances.

2 With right sides together, stitch the organza-trimmed front bodice to back bodice pieces at shoulder and side edges. Press side seams open; press shoulder seams towards back. Repeat with other front and back bodice pieces; this is the lining. Snip lining armhole seam allowances and press them to the wrong side.

3 Work a line of gathering stitches along the top curved edge of each sleeve. In the centre of the fabric piece work another line of stitches perpendicular to the first line, leaving long thread ends. Turn under and stitch a tiny hem on the remaining curved edge. With right sides facing, join underarm sleeve seams; trim seam allowances close to stitching.

4 Draw up gathers, so that sleeve is about 4–5 cm ($1^1/_2$–2 in) deep. Using a sewing needle, fasten thread ends securely with a few stitches on the underside.

stitch front and back bodice pieces at shoulder and side edges

5 Place sleeve in bodice armhole with right sides facing and with raw edges and side and underarm seams matching. Pull up gathers to fit armhole. Pin, tack and stitch in place. Snip seam allowances and press both towards bodice.

6 Place bodice and bodice lining together with right sides facing. Pin and stitch along centre back and neck edges. Turn lined bodice right side out and press, making sure stitching lies along edges.

7 Turn in the pressed seam allowances on lining armholes, and slipstitch these neatly over previously joined sleeve/armhole seam.

8 Using large zigzag stitch and leaving some space for popper on upper left edge, attach sequin strip to neckline edge.

Skirt and petticoat

1 Place one satin petticoat facing, wrong side up, on work surface. Lay one net skirt piece on top, with lower edge of satin piece extending approximately 1 cm ($^3/_8$ in). Pin pieces together, then turn lower edge of satin over lower edge of net; press. Topstitch close to folded edge. Repeat with other facing and net skirt section.

2 Join two net skirt sections together along side edge, with satin facings inside; turn right side out. Repeat with satin skirt pieces. At upper edge of satin facing, stitch through both satin and net; add another line of stitching 1 cm ($^3/_8$ in) below the first, to make a casing.

3 Place white net skirt inside satin skirt, with seams and waist edges aligned. For centre back opening, make a small cut, approximately 4 cm ($1^1/_2$ in) at centre of waistline edge of one section. Zigzag-stitch close to edges of cut, through both fabrics, reinforcing stitching at bottom of cut. Press edges to wrong side.

4 Using the longest machine stitch, work two lines of gathering, 1 cm ($^3/_8$ in) apart, across the top edge of both skirts, from one centre back edge to the other. Pull both bobbin threads to gather up the skirt to fit waist edge of bodice. Knot thread ends together, and adjust gathers evenly.

5 Pin and tack bodice and combined skirt and petticoat together, matching side seams and centre back edges. Stitch. Trim seam allowances and press them upwards.

6 Sew popper fasteners to bodice at neckline, waist and halfway between. Cut a small hole in net at casing, and insert flexible boning through casing; join ends with a few hand stitches.

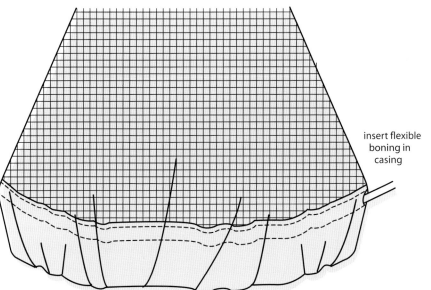

insert flexible
boning in
casing

7 Fold up lower edges of satin skirt at sides, centre front and centre back, forming a few pleats; secure with a few hand stitches. Cut four lengths of ribbon, about 40 cm (16 in) each. Tie each into a bow, and stitch in place over pleats.

8 Join centre front seam of organza top skirt. Using longest machine stitch, work two lines of stitching 1 cm ($^3/_8$ in) apart around the waist. Work two more lines of gathering down the centre front seam and to each side of the centre back opening. Pull bobbin threads to create gathers, and knot thread ends together to secure.

9 Stitch one edge of purple ribbon over gathered edge of organza top skirt. Tie ribbon around waist of dress, and secure in a bow at the back.

Complete the outfit

Finish the costume with a princess tiara.

Crazy chef

What's cooking? It could be anything, when this culinary wizard puts on his checked trousers and imposing chef's hat! Bon appétit!

Equipment

sewing machine

sewing needle

scissors

pinking shears

white and black thread

pins

craft glue

Materials

Top

1.5 m of 140 cm (1³⁄₄ yd of 55 in) wide white cotton

1 cm (³⁄₈ in) wide white bias binding: 50 cm (⁵⁄₈ yd)

6 large white buttons

1 popper fastener

Trousers

1.5 m of 112 cm (1³⁄₄ yd of 44 in) wide black and white checked cotton

2.5 cm (1 in) wide elastic: 50 cm (20 in)

Hat

60 cm of 112 cm (⁵⁄₈ yd of 44 in) wide white felt

Scarf

piece of black and white checked cotton, 65 x 25 cm (25 x 10 in)

Ready-made items

black shoes

wooden spoon/other kitchen utensils

How quick?

2 hrs 45 mins

Time saver

Purchase chef's hat.

Little helpers

Let the chef choose (within reason!) his own selection of kitchen utensils to complement the outfit.

To make

Trace Crazy Chef patterns 1, 2, 20, 37, 38 and 44 from pattern sheet, according to your child's age. Note that 1.5 cm (⁵⁄₈ in) seam allowance has been included on all pattern pieces, apart from chef's hat, which has a 1 cm (³⁄₈ in) seam allowance.

Tunic top

1 Using white cotton, make a basic tunic with back opening (see page 14).

2 Hand-stitch white buttons to front of garment, placing three to either side of centre front as shown in photograph.

Trousers

Using checked fabric, make a pair of basic trousers (see page 15).

Hat

1 Fold white felt in half crossways and pin one side hat piece (pattern 37) on a fold and cut out. Repeat, so that you have two side pieces. Cut out one brim piece (pattern 38), also on the fold. From a single thickness of the remaining fabric, cut one crown piece (pattern 44).

2 Press knife pleats in the side sections as indicated on pattern piece and in illustration (right). Stitch pleats in place, 5 mm (¹⁄₄ in) from each edge.

3 Lay one pleated side piece on top of the other, and stitch side edges to make a ring. Press seam allowances to one side, in direction of pleats.

press folds to one side to make knife pleats in hat side piece

4 Turn pleated ring wrong side out. Place crown against one edge. Pin and tack together with right sides facing. With pleated side piece on top, machine-stitch side and crown together. Turn hat right side out.

5 With right sides together, fold brim in half crossways and stitch short ends together to make a ring. Press seam open. With right sides together and centre seams matching, stitch brim to pleated section, taking 1 cm (³/₈ in) seam allowance. Turn hat brim right side out.

Scarf

Press under and stitch a narrow hem around all edges of the piece of black and white checked fabric.

Complete the outfit

Add black shoes and some kitchen utensils.

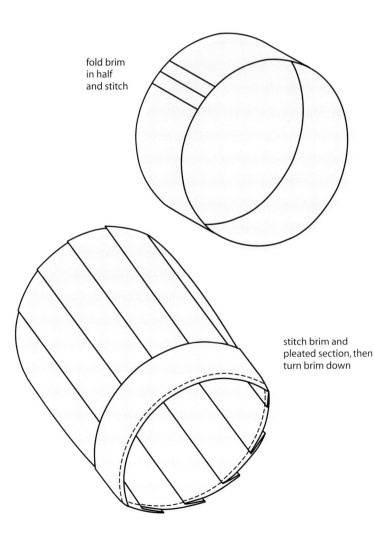

fold brim in half and stitch

stitch brim and pleated section, then turn brim down

Scarecrow

The older the materials in this simple costume, the better! For a dishevelled effect, leave raw edges on the basic tunic and trousers and add scraps of fabric and raffia.

Equipment

sewing machine

sewing needle

scissors

pinking shears

green, brown and black thread

thick brown thread

pins

hole punch

large container for dyeing fabric

Materials

Top

1.5 m of 140 cm (1³/₄ yd of 55 in) wide green and white woven-check cotton

1 popper fastener

strands of raffia/garden string

piece of old rope, 1.5 m (1³/₄ yd) long

Trousers

1.5 m of 112 cm (1³/₄ yd of 44 in) wide unbleached calico

brown fabric dye

2.5 cm (1 in) wide elastic: 50 cm (⁵/₈ yd)

scraps of bright-coloured fabric

strands of raffia/garden string

Scarf

piece of red and white spotted fabric, 50 x 50 cm (20 x 20 in)

Nose

piece of orange felt, 13 x 10 cm (5 x 4 in)

shirring elastic: 30 cm (³/₈ yd)

Ready-made items

scruffy old straw hat

oversized old boots (optional)

How quick?

2 hrs (not including time for fabric dye to dry)

Time savers

Buy a ready-made carrot nose from a fancy-dress shop.

Use previously dyed brown fabric for trousers.

Little helpers

Encourage your obliging child to get his/her hands and face dirty to enhance the scarecrow look.

To make

Trace Scarecrow template from page 142 and photocopy to enlarge to 100 per cent. Trace patterns 1, 2 and 20 from pattern sheet, according to your child's age and height. Note that 1.5 cm ($^5/_8$ in) seam allowance has been included on all pattern pieces, apart from the nose template, which has 1 cm ($^3/_8$ in) seam allowance.

Tunic

1 Using green and white checked fabric, make a basic tunic with back opening (see page 14). Leave edges, including neck, raw.

2 Using pinking shears, cut jagged points on sleeve and lower tunic edges.

3 Stitch a few strands of raffia to the wrong side of sleeve edges.

Trousers

1 Dye unbleached calico with the brown fabric dye. Leave fabric to dry.

2 Using brown fabric, make a pair of basic trousers (see page 15). Leave edges raw.

3 Cut patches, 10 x 10 cm (4 x 4 in) from bright-coloured scraps of fabric. Zigzag-stitch them to trousers. Add a couple of long straight stitches to edges of patches, using thick brown thread.

4 Stitch a few strands of raffia to the wrong side of trouser edges.

Scarf

Press under and stitch a narrow hem around all edges of the square of red and white spotted fabric.

Nose

1 Using template on page 142, pin nose piece onto orange felt and cut out.

2 Using black thread, stitch along horizontal lines where indicated on pattern, to suggest carrot ridges. Overlap long edges and stitch together to form a cone shape.

3 Punch a hole on either side of cone. Cut shirring elastic and thread through holes. Knot one end and try nose on child. Knot other end and trim off excess.

Complete the outfit

Tie the rope around the Scarecrow's waist, and tie lower edges of sleeves and trousers with lengths of raffia or garden string to add shape. Complete the look with a scruffy straw hat and oversized boots.

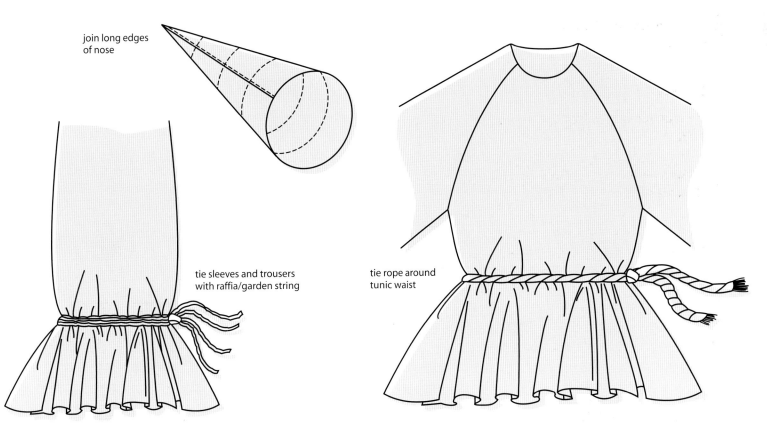

join long edges of nose

tie sleeves and trousers with raffia/garden string

tie rope around tunic waist

Templates

All templates are shown at 50 per cent. Before using, photocopy to enlarge (by 200 per cent) to 100 per cent.

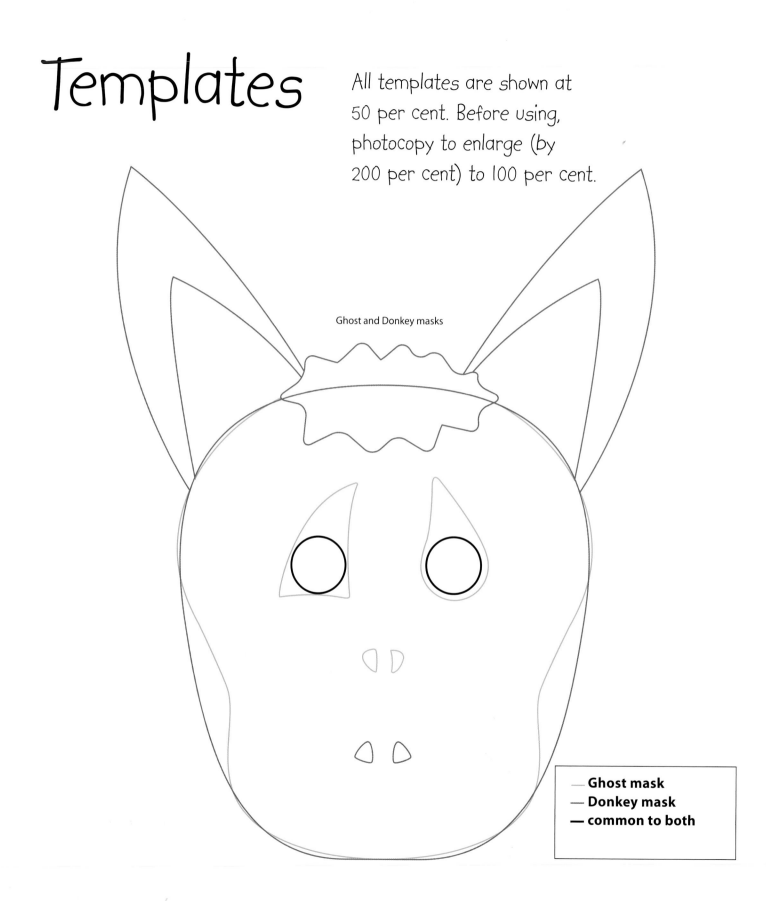

Ghost and Donkey masks

— Ghost mask
— Donkey mask
— **common to both**

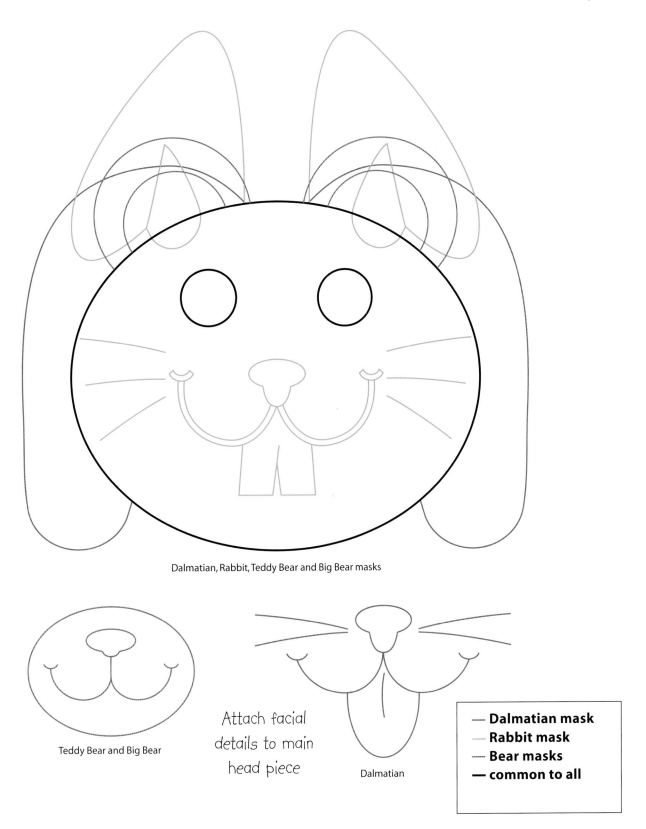

Dalmatian, Rabbit, Teddy Bear and Big Bear masks

Teddy Bear and Big Bear

Attach facial details to main head piece

Dalmatian

— **Dalmatian mask**
— **Rabbit mask**
— **Bear masks**
— **common to all**

All templates are shown at 50 per cent. Before using, photocopy to enlarge (by 200 per cent) to 100 per cent.

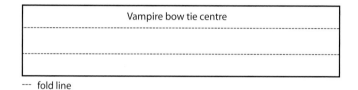

Vampire bow tie

--- fold line

Vampire bow tie centre

--- fold line

--- stitch

○ attach elastic

Scarecrow nose

Pirate eye patch

Dalmatian name tag

Pirate waistcoat detail

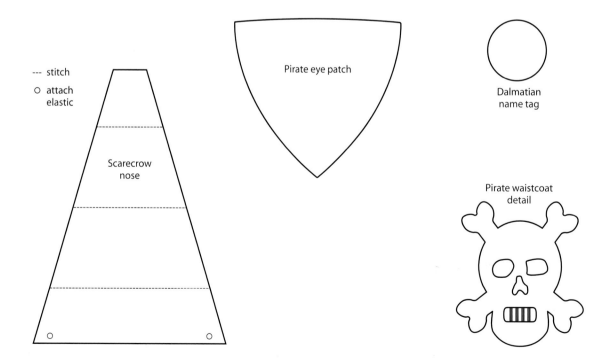

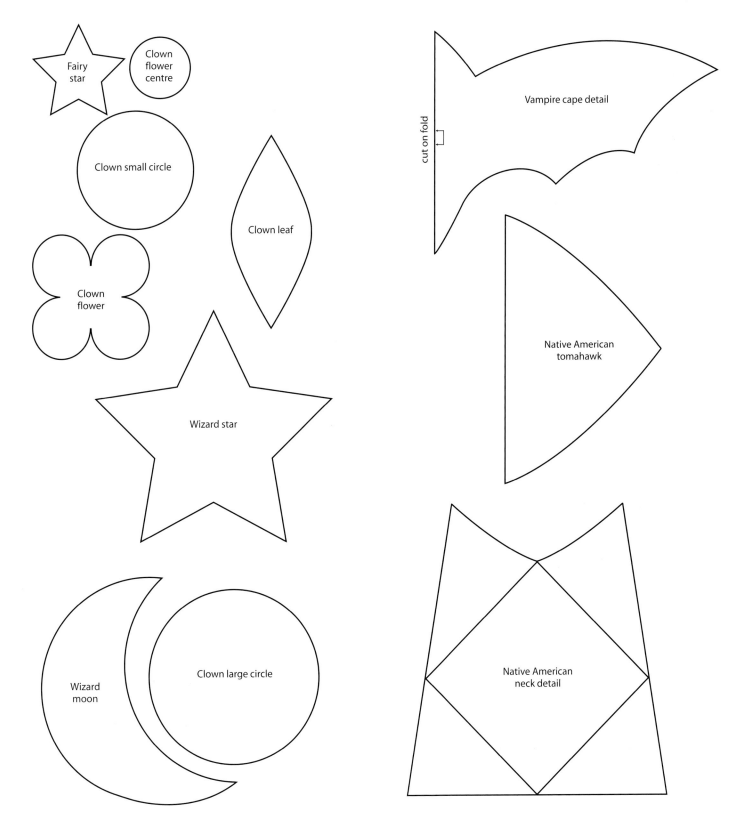

Fairy star

Clown flower centre

Clown small circle

Clown leaf

Clown flower

Wizard star

Wizard moon

Clown large circle

cut on fold

Vampire cape detail

Native American tomahawk

Native American neck detail

Index

Acknowledgements

Author's acknowledgements
With special thanks to Helen Guy-Williams
for turning my designs into such wonderful
costumes and to all the models, especially
Amelia House and Joseph Higgins, for their
hard work during the photography.

Publishers' acknowledgements
The publishers would like to thank all the
children who were photographed for this
book: Amelia House, Charlie Roberts,
Charlotte Lee, Ella Haywood, Jake Coleman,
Jemma Austin, Joseph Higgins, Kieran
Coleman, Lauren Taylor, Louis Goff, Nina
Roscoe, Ross Taylor and Shelagh Gordon.
Thanks also to Angi Woodcock for drawing
up the patterns.

Executive Editor Katy Denny
Editor Kate Tuckett, Fiona Robertson
Executive Art Editor Leigh Jones
Designer Peter Crump
Illustrator Debbie House
Costumes Helen Guy-Williams
Pattern sheet Angi Woodcock
Senior Production Controller Manjit Sihra